HOW I WAS FORCED TO BECOME A STAUNCH RACIST!

Sharmin Ali

ISBN 978-93-52019-90-8
Copyright © Sharmin Ali, 2018

First published in India 2018 by Inkstate Books
An imprint of Leadstart Publishing Pvt Ltd

Sales Office:
Unit No.25-26, Building No.A/1,
Near Wadala RTO,
Wadala (East), Mumbai – 400037 India
Phone: +91 96 99933000
Email: info@leadstartcorp.com
www.leadstartcorp.com

Disclaimer: The Views expressed in this book are those of the Author and do not pertain to be held by the Publisher.

Editor: Tanzeel Saiyed
Cover: Perspectiwitty
Layouts: Logiciels Info Solutions Pvt. Ltd.

Printed at Dhote Offset

What People Have To Say About The Book:

"The writing is exquisite! Definitely packed with suspense and the tangles with her personal life experiences make this book a true pleasure to read. Personally, enjoyed the parallelism between her personal stories and lessons learned which apply to absolutely everyonevery much."

– Margarita Faikh,
Founder, Botanicah

About the Author

Sharmin is an entrepreneur, speaker and an award-winning writer. She hails from a very humble background with strong values yet very broad horizons. She describes herself as a storyteller and a constant learner with a liberal mindset. She is a voracious reader and reads about three to four new books every month. Her writing is a direct portrayal of her learnings from life and she is mostly keen on writing about real issues that make a difference to humanity. The innumerable newspaper articles and talks that she's been a part of are not enough to read her mind. Although she enjoys a hefty internet footprint, however, it's only ten percent of her personality. Her life is more of an open book yet the real mystery unfolds through this book. The reader would get to see a very unique side to her and be amazed by her enigma to depict such simple thoughts with great authority. She tries to take the reader's mind on a roller coaster ride, filled with some great revelations about life. Whether she has succeeded or not, only time will tell, however, the reader cannot be frivolous because he/ she would be prone to some staunch racism throughout the book. The only attempt should be to just sit back, read and pass on this message to a fellow reader:

"Mediocrity is the only sin, this one life you should exercise extreme passion, utmost integrity and acute gluttony to self-discovery." **- Sharmin Ali**

Contents

Foreword

Akash Khurana, Ph.D.

Bollywood Actor, Director, HR Developer, Corporate Leader, Screenwriter.

The first time I met Sharmin Ali was in Bengaluru when she had come to watch a performance of Vijay Tendulkar's A Friend's Story, a play directed by me. This was one of our earlier runs, and we were still unsure of how much my intent was getting through to audiences. Her feedback was gratifying and inspiring. We got on a small chat and it turned out I had already read about her plays on Facebook on one of the groups. She had performed a blasphemous play (written by herself) a few months before and I couldn't stop wondering about the gutsy concept the play carried. Although I didn't watch the play, but getting to meet her after that was quite interesting because frankly I would never dare perform such staunch plays. And that was that.

Then, out of the blue, after over a year, I get this surprising message from her asking me if I would write the Foreword for her new book.

My obvious question: "Why me?" Her enigmatic response: "I've thought long and hard about it. Why not you?" And that was that.

You may say that's not reason enough to consider a cold call, and yet I acceded to her request. As I write this, I ask myself why I agreed to do this. A line from the autobiographical play 'Tuesdays with Morrie' flashes through my mind: When author Mitch Albom's wife Janine is invited by his professor Morrie Schwartz to visit him, despite Albom's reluctance, she accepts. When Mitch asks her, what made her say yes to him, Janine simply said, "he asked me." Well, Sharmin asked me.

But on a more serious note, the material she sent me to read was a revelation: Sharmin Ali is a polymath who has diligently pursued diverse vocations. And in this book, she has empathetically applied her own experiential learnings in evolving a new paradigm of life skills for young Indian leaders in the world of corporates and start-ups.

While offering her own take on what being successful means, she helps you explore how far you would go in your quest for the Holy Grail of Success, and then consequently suggests values that might help you along in achieving your goals.

Enigmatic as it may sound, 'How I was forced to become a staunch RACIST!' attempts to establish each individual's self-awareness of how unique and special one can be amidst the ever-growing multitudes, without the fear of despondency.

In fact, the curious nature of the book's audacious title sets up an intriguing prism through which the reader may be led on new pathways to self-discovery.

Dedication

To Ma, Baba and Rusha…

To YOU...

I.
STRUGGLE

- The Journey of My Life

I belong to a Kolkata-based family. My father is a geo-scientist and works with the public sector and my mother is a lawyer by profession, though she quit practice a long time ago. My father's job rendered me a multi-cultural childhood since his job required him to switch cities from time-to time. However, I have spent the maximum time of my childhood in the bountiful state of Gujarat. For my parents, the greatest gift of God is education. **My greatest homework** during summer vacations was studying and preparing for the next semester in school. While my friends would be camping, playing sports, swimming, travelling to far-off destinations, I would only be drooling over curriculum-based books. My summer-break assignments from school were always the best and my grades were always A+. Thanks to my Baba! He is the most disciplined, dedicated and punctual man on this planet with such impeccable mannerisms that I always wondered how he became a scientist and didn't join the army, for he is the best suited for that.

During the 12 years in Ahmedabad, **my greatest escapade** was my 5-day swimming session! When I was in the fifth grade at school, my baba finally decided to put me into a summer camp that imparted swimming lessons to kids. One fine summer morning, baba walked up to my bed and said, "Get ready in 15 minutes. We are going out." For the first time in 10 years, I was super thrilled for we were going out in the morning rather than the usual morning study time. I jumped from my 6 by 4 feet luxurious bed and rushed into the bathroom, wore my best dress and got ready in 15 minutes with the fear that if I got late, baba might just cancel the plan. I was so delighted at the fact that we were going out at 9 am that I drank a whole glass of milk Ma gave in one breath and ran. For someone who hated milk, this definitely was an achievement. I went down to the parking lot where our white-coloured, second-hand Maruti 800 was parked. I got into the car and we drove off. If you had been with me, you would have experienced the most adventurous, exciting and curiosity-driven ride of your life at 9 am of a hot summer morning in June, in a Maruti 800. I constantly kept asking baba about where we were going for I couldn't control my suppressed curiosity anymore. He just kept quiet and being the very careful driver that he is, just quietly drove. After about 20 minutes, baba stopped at a junction, parked the car and asked me to step out. I quietly obliged.

'Shah & Shah Bhai Swimming Classes'

At the tender age of 10, I was not aware about ecstasy or any other form of drugs. But if there were a virtual drug that could make you feel ecstatic for a moment, I possibly had consumed it in my mind! The unbelievably unexpected had just taken shape. *"Aamra ekhane ki korchi baba? (What are we doing here, baba?)"* I asked. Baba promptly replied, "Follow me." Have you ever felt goose bumps in your stomach or have you ever looked down from a hill top and felt like jumping down? That was the sensation in my entire body. We lived in Chandkheda, Ahmedabad and the swimming classes were held at Ramnagar which was about 3 kilometres away from my house. We walked to a registration counter and baba bought a package and handed over to me. He filled in a form, paid the fees and we walked in. Had you been with me, you would have seen an approximately 100-feet area divided into two pools with blue-coloured chlorinated water. The first pool read: '6 FEET DEPTH! CAUTION! CHILDREN NOT ALLOWED!' We walked to the second pool. A dark, tall and stout looking man stood in a fluorescent-orange underwear. His shocking loud voice and the shocking orange underwear aptly coincided with his body language. He was yelling at a group of boys in Gujarati, *"Ehh, shoo kari che tame log?* (What are you boys doing?)"* I soon realised that this orange man was our swimming instructor 'Shah bhai'. Baba introduced me to him. He asked baba to go stand in the waiting area behind the pool. I was told to go change into my swimming costume that baba gave me in the package. I came out in five minutes dressed in a shocking orange swimming costume! It seemed like I was about to jump in orange water and the world suddenly started appearing orange to me! The instructor asked me to jump inside the pool and like my baba always taught me to not listen to strangers and to use your own reasoning before doing anything, I said, "I don't know how to swim, I won't jump." He said that the pool wasn't deep and that nothing would happen to me. After great amounts of refusal, he finally pulled me in and I screamed AAAAAAGGGGGGGH!!!!!!!!!!!!!

The water was quite cold and heavily chlorinated. My shocking orange swimsuit reflected clearly in the clear blue water. I later understood that baba bought that colour to spot me from among the close to 100 children in that pool. Of course, he was going to closely notice my progress and take regular status updates from the instructor! The first day was just jumping around and playing in the water. The actual training started from the second day when he taught us how to kick the water and glide like a mermaid. I tried my best to learn gliding in the two-hour session but somehow I wasn't getting it right. Baba screamed from the waiting area, "Follow the other children. What are you doing? If they can do it, why can't you?" The shocking orange on me suddenly became the centre of attraction for everyone. This followed the next day again and my baba lost it for the second time. He went and spoke to the instructor for 15 minutes and it seemed like the instructor got belted. By the fourth day, a majority of children had mastered the art of gliding and I was still not even half as close. Baba suddenly yelled in Hindi, "*Abey, kya kar raha hai tu? Usko sikha jaldi!* (Hey, what are you doing? Teach her fast!) I was so embarrassed that I didn't dare to turn around and look at the sudden fame again. All I remember was that the very next moment I was drowning in the water for five seconds! I came up and go again! Five seconds in the water! Come up and go again! Five seconds in the water for a third time in a row! CHODO! CHODO! CHODO! BACHAO! BACHAO! BACHAO! BABA HELP ME! BABA…BABA… What had just happened? The instructor was so angry at my father that he lifted me upside down and threw me into the water for three continuous times. My father yelled, "*Haan achche se sikha usko!*"

I WAS COMPLETELY JOLTED!!!!!

The fifth day was an exact revision of the fourth with me unable to learn anything. I was so frightened and scared of the water that I stayed in one corner and didn't even dare to look up at my father. All I remember next was that my father withdrew me from the swimming classes.

THE END OF AN ESCAPADE! THE END OF AN EXPERIENCE! THE END OF ECSTASY!

Lesson learnt: To get noticed, you have to be shocking, bold and controversial!

Have you ever almost gotten killed? Have you ever seen death twice and just managed to escape it? Have you ever been forced onto a weighing scale to question the reason for your existence?

If you had been with me on the 28th of February 2002, you would have been completely shaken up by the most gruesome and despicable act on humanity ever. I woke up with the news of the Godhra riots having broken out in Gujarat. Little did I know that at the very playful age of 12, I would be forced to see the most terrible incident of my life. For the first time ever, I saw my father cry. Had you been with me, you would have experienced 25.7 kilometres of sheer misery: the scariest road trip that I have ever taken in my life in the middle of the night in an ambulance with rattling glasses. I suddenly heard an old man croon a tune, "Twinkle twinkle little star, how I wonder what you are. Oh God, if only we could make it alive would I truly believe that you are, you are, you are… Twinkle twinkle little star…" I along with my parents and a 6-year-old sister and a number of other families were being rescued from the horrendous riots and being transported to the airport at 2:30 a.m. in an ambulance. My heart sank as we finally reached the airport. It was indeed my tryst with destiny.

Exactly a year before, Gujarat was struck with the biggest natural disaster ever. Had you been with me on the 26th of January 2001, you would have witnessed multi-storeyed buildings fall apart like a mere pack of cards. Gujarat was struck by an earthquake of 8.9 Richter scale, rendering a million homeless and killing thousands of people. We spent the next two months in a rehabilitation camp.

Lesson learnt: If life gives you a second chance, take it! And if it gives you a third, you better be fair!

Have you ever met any negative person in your life? Have you ever been insulted in public? Can one incident decide the course of your career?

I AM IMPERFECT! I AM IMPERFECT! I AM IMPERFECT!

8th of August 1997 at 2 p.m. of a windy afternoon, if you had been with me, you would have seen me returning from school in a navy blue-coloured Maruti van stuffed with at least thirty children and driven by our very stout, petite and miserly, Patel Bhai. Suddenly, one of my Gujarati friends Aadil Lokhandwala popped out from the hustle and said something. I couldn't pay attention to what he said so I asked, "Could you please repeat that?" to which the most horrific reply ever was, "I know you can't talk properly, at least listen! Go clean your ears!"

MY SPINE FROZE…

My long-kept secret had just come out. Yes, I had a terrible stammering problem as a kid, an unfortunate handicap that I couldn't really do much about. I was so ashamed and disappointed with all the whispering, mocking and staring that I didn't go to school for the next three days!

I was so distraught that I decided to never open my mouth in public again. The greatest gift that we humans possess is the power to communicate through language. How I wished I were an animal with no such capacity! The more you try to suppress your hunger, the hungrier you feel.

I was always very attracted to the world of theatre, plays, drama, nautanki and the likewise.

If you had been with me on the 25th of December 1997, you would have seen me on live on stage performing for the very well-known English play Cinderella. If you are thinking that how a girl with a speech defect could play the role of the beautiful Cinderella, then please do not race your horses, because I did not. Of course not! With great difficulty, I had got the role of one of the princess' maids. Thanks to my Ma's repeated calling up to our drama teacher Mr. Surinder Bhalla and requesting him to just give me one chance! I promised to not let him down.

On Stage: Prince is dancing with Cinderella-Clock strikes midnight- Cinderella runs-leaves her shoe behind-Runs and runs and runs until she reaches home-And there she is back to the green room to change to her rags. Prince is on stage and looks around for Cinderella.

Stage opens to the next scene: Step mother calls out for Cinderella!

Cinderella! Cinderella! Cinderella! Come out you girl! Where are you?

Ideally Cinderella should have come out immediately.

Cinderella! Cinderella! Cinderella! Come out you girl! Where are you?

Still no sign of Cinderella!

Cinderella! Cinderella! Cinderella! Come out you girl! Where are you?

Backstage fury: Where is Cinderella?

I don't know Sir, I don't know Sir, I don't know either… Cinderella! Cinderella! Cinderella! Come out you girl!

Where are you?

By now, the step mother had already forgotten her next line and Mr. Bhalla had lost his temper completely! He yelled at the green room, "Dress up any girl in rags and just send her on stage!"

Cinderella! Cinderella! Cinderella! Come out you girl! Where are you?

Yes, moooooo….ther….Wwwwwwww…..hat is it? Hhhhhh….ow can I help?

Get me my tea immediately before I lose it completely!

All I remember next is that Mr. Bhalla and the original Cinderella came and thanked me for my spontaneity! (Just for the record: She had slipped in the bathroom and fallen, so she couldn't make it to the stage, giving me an opportunity to prove my latent calibre!)

Lesson learnt: Imperfection is beauty. Madness is genius. It is better to be absolutely ridiculous than absolutely boring!

BANSAL, KOTA Vs. DPS RK PURAM, NEW DELHI

One decision that changed the course of my life forever…

The biggest advantage of being born to a family working in the public sector is that you get to travel a lot. Because of my father's transferrable job, we got to travel to a lot of places. So, I had the opportunity to spend a few years amidst the beautiful valley of Assam. After completing my

10th grade board exams, I had a 2-month break. Of course, my potentially studious family decided to do something fruitful yet again. But this time, the catalyst was an external force for a change.

One day, Ma's best friend Jharna auntie visited us with her family. Her elder son, Shibu was the next Einstein in the making. *(For the record: This is what Jharna auntie told us.)* If you had been with me, you would have seen a five feet 3 inches' boy with soda glasses and hair as short and fine as a porcupine's. Shibu dada, as I called him *(dada in Bengali refers to an elder brother, used to show respect)* seemed to be continuously caught in his thoughts. Jharna auntie, dressed in a *laal par* saree (saree with a red border), undoubtedly every Bengali woman's favourite, and a tremendously huge red bindi upon her forehead seemed to be carving her potato-like face and two rasgulla-like cheeks in a pretty ecstatic way.

"So, Bonnie, what is your ambition in life?" Jharna auntie asked.

Ummmm…. *(I was pondering)*

"IIT or AIIMS?" she barked!

"Jani na, dekhi, duto hi debo, jekhane hoye jabe, shekhane jabo…" (I don't know, let's see, I'll take both the exams, will pursue whatever I get through) I said in a very ginger tone.

"What are you saying? How can you still not decide on one? Your exams are over! It's high time! OK, SO I'LL TELL YOU WHAT YOU SHOULD DO! Start preparing for Bansal exams from tonight. Your grades are pretty good, so it shouldn't be difficult for you. Take the exam in June and then join the Engineering prep classes there! Study very hard for two years and then crack IIT! I want to see you in IIT Kharagpur as Shibu's junior! He's going to crack the IIT very soon. If you need any help, he will guide you! Shibu, why don't you give her some tips?" she commanded!

"***
****
****
****
****
****
***"

I abused her left, right, centre, top, bottom and every other dimension possible, in my head.

WHO THE HELL IS JHARNA AUNTIE TO DECIDE MY

CAREER????????

After a two-day dharna at home, I finally decided to at least take the Bansal test. The test took place on the 10th of May and I wasn't expecting it to get converted. After a week-long stint at home, the board exam results were finally declared and I had secured a 90%.

One of my neighbours told me that she was applying to DPS RK Puram, New Delhi with her board exam percentage and if selected, she would be called for an interview. Assam was undergoing huge insurgent attacks during the same period and it was becoming increasingly unsafe. Also, pursuing higher education was a problem due to several political reasons. So, I decided to apply to DPS RK Puram, New Delhi. After having finished the application, I had to get a final signature from my Principal, so I went to school to get the formalities completed. As soon as the Principal was about to sign, suddenly my father walked in.

"Sharmin, you have been selected at Bansal, Kota for IIT training!!!"

BANSAL, KOTA OR DPS RK PURAM, NEW DELHI???

FATHER: KOTA, KOTA, KOTA MOTHER: KOTA, KOTA, KOTA

JHARNA AUNTIE: MY SON WILL HELP YOU, GO TO KOTA

ME: DPS RK PURAM, NEW DELHI!!!!!

I had the two best years of my life.

11th Grade: 60% secured (30% drop from 10th!) – Parents freaked out – At the verge of withdrawing me from DPS – Mom, dad, Jharna auntie and the entire world Vs. Me – I will not leave DPS!

End of two years: IIT gone! AIIMS gone! Jharna auntie's friendship gone! Parents disappointed! Incredible student-faculty relationship achieved! Amazing batch mates achieved! India habitat centre, Siri fort, Kamani auditorium checked! Javed Akhtar, Shabana Azmi, Sharmila Tagore performances checked! The value of independence, interdependence, intelligence achieved! Immense personality growth achieved! Definitely worth the investment!

Lesson Learnt: Rebellion is the world's greatest trigger! Be rebellious and write your own destiny!

HADOOP! PIG! HIVE! R! SAS! SQL! EXCEL!

Below are a few snippets revolving around what I did for two long years of my life:

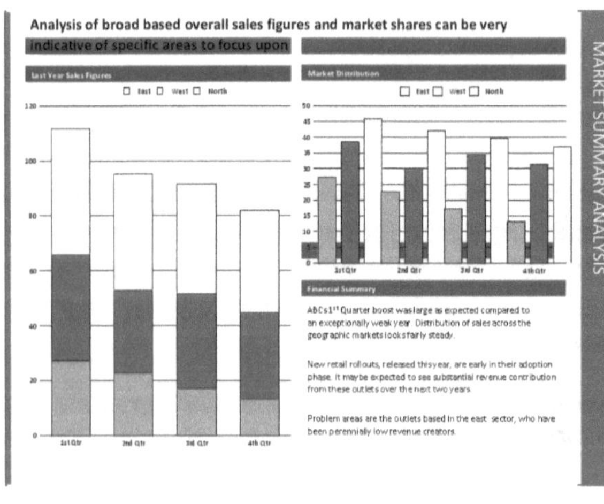

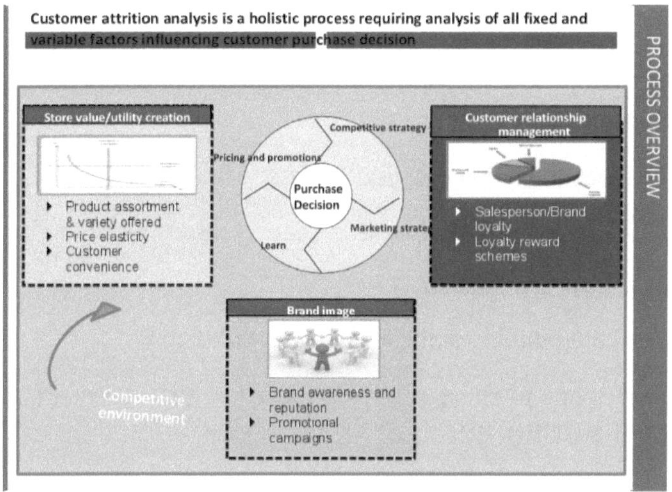

For those of you who are wondering that Latin makes more sense than these words, this is exactly what I thought when I heard of them for the very first time!

Welcome to the world of Big Data, Consulting & Analytics!

After completing my Engineering degree, I was placed with a consulting firm delivering business solutions to Fortune 100 companies, helping enlarge their businesses and grow their sales. We had to literally invest 14-15 hours in a day at work. At times, weekends would also be spent at the office. I would get back home at 3 a.m. and wake up at 7 a.m. ONLY to take con-calls. 24x7 HOURS OF CLAUSTROPHOBIA!!!!!

After completing almost one and half years, during one of our appraisal cycles, my manager called me to a cabin to discuss my performance report. He showed me a slide with the below pointers:

1. Performance: **D**

2. Project Deliverables: **C**

3. New projects/PPOs: **D**

4. Documentation of work: **D**

5. Manager Satisfaction: **D**

6. Client Satisfaction: **A**

7. Team building skills/Knowledge Sharing: **B**

F*** YOU F*** YOU F*** YOU F*** YOU F*** YOU F*** YOU!!!!!!!!!!!

I was so insanity-struck that I just stormed off from the room and banged the door on his face! What the hell had just happened?

I was so dejected that I didn't go to work for the next three days. All I received was an email from the HR manager that I would be placed on a PIP (Personal Improvement Plan) for the next three months to monitor my performance and that my manager would guide me on how to become a responsible employee for further promotions. In case I failed to deliver, I would be relieved of my duties with a 15-day notice period!

ARE YOU SERIOUSLY KIDDING ME? DO I HAVE NO SAY IN MY CAREER? WHO ARE YOU TO DECIDE MY CAPACITY TO DELIVER?

I cleared the program with an A and finished all the tasks I was assigned. Next, I called for a meeting with the HR head, the senior manager and my manager. I was asked to present my learnings in the last three months. I gave a larger than life presentation, followed by a slide which read the following:

"ANY QUESTIONS?"

The senior manager praised me so much that his only question was, "Why didn't you perform like this before?"

I was silent. I just clicked the 'Page Down' button on my laptop.

"YOU DON'T DESERVE MY SERVICES ANYMORE!

SO, I RELIEVE YOU FROM GIVING ME ANY FURTHER PROMOTIONS! ALL THE BEST!"

Lesson Learnt: Fire Your Boss To Grow Big In Life!

THE GIRL STORE

- I am not for profit...

"Women are systematically degraded by receiving the trivial attentions which men think it manly to pay to the sex, when, in fact, men are insultingly supporting their own superiority."

"To be a good mother — a woman must have sense, and that independence of mind which few women possess are taught to depend entirely on their husbands. Meek wives are, in general, foolish mothers; wanting their children to love them best, and take their part, in secret, against the father, who is held up as a scarecrow"....... *Mary Wollstonecraft, Vindication of the Rights of Women (1790)*

These words come from a woman who belonged to an era where women were treated as mere toys in medieval Europe. She was highly critical of the contemporary attitudes to women and fought for their rights. She later became a philosopher and is best known for her book 'Vindication of the Rights of Women' which paved the way for hundreds of women in Britain to fight for their rights. Her daughter continued tradition and became famous for her popular work titled 'Frankestein'.

"Dead Negroes tell no tales!" .... *Harriet Tubman (1850s)*

Can you gauge the audacity in this one remark? Harriet Tubman better known as *the Moses of the Black* became famous as a "conductor" on the Underground Railroad during the turbulent 1850s in America. Born a slave on Maryland's eastern shore, she endured the harsh existence of a field hand, including brutal beatings. In 1849 she fled slavery, leaving her husband and family behind in order to escape. Despite a bounty on her head, she returned to the South at least 19 times to lead her family and hundreds of other slaves to freedom via the Underground Railroad. Tubman also served as a scout, spy and nurse during the Civil War.

"The best things in the world are free. The second-best things are very expensive." .... *Coco Chanel (1920)*

A classic example of a revolutionary!

Up until the First World War, women's clothing had been quite restrictive and tended to involve full length skirts which were impractical for many activities. Coco Chanel helped create women's clothing that was simpler and more practical. She also introduced trousers and suits for women – something which had not been done before. She later revolutionised women's clothing and gave birth to one of the world's most loved and most expensive brands!

I have been extremely fortunate to have met one woman who according to me has been a great example of indignance. *(Name has been kept anonymous on request.)* Her story is every common woman's story, the brutality that she underwent in her marriage is something extremely common to a lot of women around the world. The brittle relationship with her husband forced her to take a decision that later changed the mark of his dynasty forever. I translated my conversation with her into a play and we staged it recently at one of my theatre shows. Below is an excerpt from the play:

(35) Tribal woman

(Dark room: Woman masturbating, makes sounds…… the sound gets louder, moans very loudly, finally cums)

Scene opens to a beautiful tribal woman…. smiling and looks very happy…

In the dark woods, under a starry sky, far away from everyone…. I was feeling my body when he saw me for the first time. Most women would get scared, try to run away or scream for help. But I did not make a sound. Just kept feeling myself and made him watch me do it. I wanted him to watch me. I was at my peak when he smiled. He had the smile of an angel. Such beautiful eyes…. what they say 'tall, dark and handsome'. Seemed like a European, I could figure out from his distinct features.

"Hello!" he said and offered his hand to me. I obliged. Aah…. that was the firmest touch ever. How I wish my husband would feel me like that all over.

"Who are you," he asked. "Kakinara," I said.

"Can I take your photograph?"

"Mine……?"

"Yes, I'm here on a photography project. I work with the national Geographic channel and we are covering the most beautiful and the most sinful destinations on this planet and right now there is nothing more sinful than you……"

"Do you mind?"

(She stares at him surprised but amused… keeps staring for a long time…. gets up, wraps her dress and starts rushing)

How dare he say that? Huh? Sorry, you are sorry… what? I am the most beautiful woman you have ever seen… you like the depth in my eyes, the touch of my hands, I feel like silk on a bare body…… (suddenly she smiles and touches him tenderly)

"What do I get in return?"

"What do I want?"

"I want you! I want your body! I want your touch! I want your warmth!..................... I want your child!"

(Long pause)

"Will you give me that? Then I will let you take my photograph."

"Okay? Did you just say okay?" (Smiles…)

(Hugs him…music in the background)

(Action for kiss, feeling and love-making and then intercourse…. with music in the background. Once they are done, she is lying in his arms).

"I am the queen of this mountain village. I was married to the king at the age of 20, fifteen years ago. He is 20 years elder to me. In our community, the king gets to marry the most beautiful girl in the village, no matter how old he is. Fifteen years of marriage and not once has he made me feel complete, so I have to do myself the favour."

(Kisses him again)

(Long pause)

"They are about to kill me! Because I have still not delivered his child. And he can't remarry until I die. But only I know the real reason for…… the no child condition…… he is incapable, you know, he is impotent…. (shows frustration and expresses her hatred for him). He doesn't want anyone to know, so he killed his first two wives and now he will kill me too if I don't give the child. But, how do I?

How do I?

How can he?

But you can…

You will…

And I will do anything you want…"

"Huhhhh….? Why can't I run away? Because then my father will get killed and our family will lose its name.

I will come to meet you every night for the next seven nights that you are here and we will make love until dawn. You can then shoot me, but at sunrise I shall leave…."

(Looks at the audience now)

"We did it for the next ten nights. And then he left. And if you are wondering how I know your language, then you must know that this was not the first time I had had a…. what do you say? Aah… an extra marital affair. How could I, a tribal queen, distinguish between races, cultures and languages? He was not my first……… but definitely the last because I truly loved him. I loved him so much that he gave me the most beautiful part of my life (picks up the child wrapped in a cloth and kisses him), my son, Steven, after his name. I love you, Steven……"

Sings her tribal song again and exits…

Lesson Learnt: A leader's greatest characteristic is the ability to create and deal with an alarming situation!

MY DEEPEST REGRET

One thousand songs in your pocket! - *iPod positioning*

World's thinnest notebook! It's so thin that it fits inside an office envelope! – *Mac Book Air positioning*

My deepest regret is that it took me so long to learn this skill! I could have saved three long years of my life if only I had known the biggest secret to running a successful business! No matter what business you have ventured into, until and unless you get the positioning statistics right, you will not succeed.

Imagine a product like an iPad. What is it that makes it so special? A device so expensive is practically offering you the same services any other cheap tablet does. Why is the iPad still so special? What is it that differentiates the iPad from an HP Slate? *Just the positioning!*

Now imagine having coffee at home and having coffee at a Starbucks outlet. Any rational person would prefer having coffee at home for it is the same coffee not even served on a golden platter! And you end up paying four times the price! Why do people still go to a Starbucks outlet? What is the biggest farce in this world? *Just the positioning!*

Have you ever cooked chicken at home? I'm sure you have or have at least seen your mom cook it. Do you know the spices that go into it? Let me name a few: Ginger, garlic, cardamom, garam masala, cumin, red chillies, coriander, etc. So here I have already named seven important spices. What do you think is so secretive about the eleven secret herbs and spices in Kentucky Fried Chicken then? *Just the positioning!*

Which is the world's most preferred drink? What was the soldier's royal drink during the World war? What has become one of the world's largest brands? A drink that contains sugar, water, cola and carbon dioxide! Research claims that it has the capacity to dissolve your teeth, harm your intestines and of course clean your toilet better than acid. Why is Coke still the number one? *Just the positioning!*

Lesson Learnt: Sell the idea, not the product.

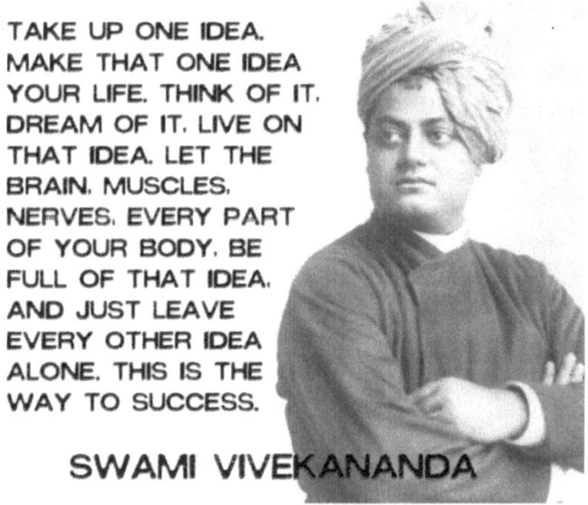

Can you imagine the amount of gravitas in these lines? An idea can be transformed into your life's biggest venture ever by following this easy technique! The power of never quitting unless you succeed is so evident in these lines. The idea of overtaking your innermost fears and inhibitions is reflecting perfectly.

My life's one and only idea:

To master the art of writing and impact a million lives by sharing my formula to write and publish your first book!

There were umpteen situations when I had completely lost patience. Imagine being jobless for two years and living on minimal resources without taking any external help. Imagine reading a hundred bestselling books only to come up with that secret to creating a masterpiece. Imagine knowing the secret yet not being able to translate it into a step-by-step formula! BRAIN-WRENCHING IMPATIENCE, RESTLESSNESS AND FRUSTRATION!

No money, no life, no friends! ONLY this one formula! You dream of it! You live with it! You sleep with it! This one formula becomes your life forever!

It took me two years to come up with my copyright formula: 'YOUR-FIRST-BOOK'! This was possible only because I was determined in doing what no author in this world has ever done!

> *"I am not trying to build a church, but a religion, a way of life!"*

I have given 24 months of my life in creating the one formula needed to write and publish your first book!

Will you give me 24 hours of your life to learn it?

Lesson Learnt: You cannot achieve anything without dedication, determination and discipline!

THE LITTLE BOY WHO EDUCATED ME

"I was born brilliant, but education spoilt me until I met this 7-year-old…"

I was once travelling from RT Nagar to Indira Nagar at 7 a.m. in the morning in an auto to get to an early morning meeting. Had you been with me, you would have experienced a freezing temperature, quite unusual for Bangalore tropical climate on a winter morning in November. I was busy googling the destination on my smart phone when suddenly the auto driver started talking.

"My seven-year-old son was playing on the terrace of our house when he suddenly tripped and fell down. He bled so much from the head that doctors fear he might go into a coma if he's not operated by tomorrow evening. The operation would cost 20,000 rupees and I need to deposit it by this evening at the NIMHANS (National Institute of Mental health and Neuro Surgery) hospital, Bangalore. My relatives have agreed to lend me 5000 rupees and after driving the auto all night, I have managed to accumulate 2000 rupees. I urgently need 13,000 rupees madam. Please tell me if you have to go anywhere else and inform your friends also. I will drive all day today and try my best to collect as much as possible. He is my only child…."

I listened to him in absolute silence. As soon as he dropped me near BDA Complex, Indira Nagar, I asked him to wait for two minutes as I was not carrying any cash to pay the auto fare. I withdrew cash from the nearest Canara bank ATM and handed it over to him.

"Go get your son treated and call me on 8861****** if you need any help."

The auto driver looked at me in complete surprise, thanked me for my generosity and left. I had just turned and started walking, when I was suddenly dawned with the most basic question: WHAT IF HE WAS LYING? DID I JUST GET ROBBED? WHAT AN EMOTIONAL STORY!!!!! I immediately turned back to look if he was still there. And he was still there counting the money I had just given him: 13,000 rupees.

"Can I have your phone number, *bhaiya*? I'll call and check once the operation is done."

"Yes madam, of course."

I tried calling him the next day to check on his son. Actually, no! I called to check if he really had cheated me or not. I wanted to prove my ego wrong and my gut right. But there was no response. I called him continuously for the next three days. No response.

YOU CHEAT! YOU TRAITOR! YOU THEIF! YOU SCOUNDREL! I WILL NEVER EVER HELP ANYONE! THIS WORLD IS FULL OF DISHONEST PEOPLE! I WAS ANGRY! VERY ANGRY!

UNTIL THE FIFTH DAY……

"Madam, I'm Asif calling, the auto driver from that day. I hope you remember me. I just wanted to say thank you Madam. My son is out of danger now. He was asking about you Madam. If you have some time, please come and meet him. He is in room 201 at the NIMHANS general ward. Thank you Madame. May Allah bless you…"

I did not say a word for the next 1 hour. I was so ashamed of myself for having cursed him so much. How could I be so terrible? How could I? I immediately rushed to the hospital, about five kilometres from my residence. As I walked into room 201, I was shocked at what I saw. If you had been with me, you would have seen a seven-year-old boy covered in bandages all over his head with a bottle of blood and glucose on either side of his thin body. I quietly sat on the iron stool next to his bed and kept looking at him.

"Hi!"

"Hello!"

"Are you the one who saved my life?"

"No, I am not the surgeon. I am Sharmin. I didn't do anything."

"Yes, you are right. Actually, not you, the auto saved my life."

"How is that?"

"See. I'll explain. We had no money. You gave us the money. Why did you give? Because you probably felt sympathetic towards my condition. Why did you feel sympathetic? Because my Abba narrated my sad story to you. Why did he narrate it to you? Because you were in the auto he was driving. So, if you go back, you will realise that actually the auto saved my life!"

I instantly had a smile on my face.

"Which school do you go to?"

"I don't go to any school. We don't have enough money."
"What do you do then?"

"I am a tourist guide at the Tipu Sultan palace in Mysore. I show the palace around to the tourists who come to visit Mysore."

"So, you work there to support your family. What about your education?"

"Oh no-no, I don't work there. I don't support my family at all. I only support my education. I am strictly against child labour. I wanted to study but we had no money so no school and we had no deposit money to avail free education. So, I decided to educate myself. I show the Tipu Sultan's palace to the tourists for one hour and when they offer to pay, I refuse to accept money. Instead, I ask them to spare one hour of their day and teach me something about their land, language, culture, history or just about anything under the sky. You see this blood and this glucose. Did you know they are both made up of carbon compounds? The difference is that blood also contains iron and other minerals in it. The doctor taught me this because Abba promised to give him a free ride in return."

For the first time in my life, I was completely bowled over by a seven-year-old and his perspectives in life!

Lesson Learnt: Impulsive decision making, spontaneity and following your gut are the characteristics of the right brain! You are a right brainer!

SELFISH TO SELFLESS

World War I, World War II, Taiping Rebellion, Mongol conquests, Vietnam, A Lushan Rebellion, Qing dynasty conquest of the Ming dynasty, Russian Civil war, Napoleonic wars, European Renaissance period

What is common among all of them?

THEY ARE ALL MAJOR LANDMARKS IN HISTORY! MILLIONS OF DEATHS! POLITICAL CONUNDRUMS! FIGHT FOR POWER! WORLD OF CAPITALISM! EXISTENTIAL CRISIS!

YES, BUT WHAT ELSE?

VIOLENCE WAS THE ONLY WAY USED TO FIGHT THEM!

NOW ANSWER THIS!

Who is the biggest outlier this country has ever produced?

MOHANDAS KARAMCHAND GANDHI

Imagine a man dressed in a single piece of cloth travelling the entire country to fight for independence with ONLY the ideology of non-violence, in a world where the hunger for power is of primary importance!

Now imagine a man born to the royal family of a rare South African tribe, becoming the greatest known personality in the world for his fight against apartheid! Imagine spending 27 long years of your life in prison only to fight for the rights of your people! Imagine giving up every God damn pleasure of your life to create an impact on the lives of billions of people around the world!

THAT IS THE POWER OF INDIGNANCE!

When Nelson Mandela became the President of South Africa, it wasn't the victory of Blacks against apartheid.

It was the victory of humanity! It proved that the common man has the power to change the world if he is indignant and audacious enough to take that one step!

Lesson Learnt: Impact is more important than fame and money!

I got up one day, looked at the mirror and said these words out loud to myself:

AUDACIOUS

BOLD

INDIGNANT

DARING

ECCENTRIC

BRAZEN

STRIKING

OUTSTANDING

HIGH-FLIER

ROBUST

PROMINENT

CLEAR

DISTINCT

SPECIFIC

POSITIONING

ALARMING

TRUSTWORTHY

ZEALOUS

IMPACTFUL

SUCCESSFUL

BEST-EST!

And I asked myself three questions:

What am I doing with my life?

If not now, when?

If not me, who?

BIGGEST LESSON I HAVE LEARNT IN MY LIFE

SCREW MEDIOCRITY!!!

II.
SEED

- The Day I Lost My Virginity

Have you ever really had an explosive orgasm? Have you ever achieved something unimaginable? Have you really lost your virginity?

I'm not a virgin!

For those of you getting ideas, hold your horses boys! As much as I love adorning a mystical wrap around myself to enslave your brain's creative juices, I shall let down the secret sauce, so you can have a breather now!

At the age of eighteen, I got a chance to present a paper on Entrepreneurship at one of the biggest paper presentation conferences at the Chowdiah Memorial hall, Bangalore. I was one of the youngest being in the first year of college to be presenting at such a prestigious event and contesting for an IEEE international recognition. I had the opportunity to meet a gentleman at the conference who was one of the chief guests for the event. This man has impacted my life in the greatest way possible. Had it not been for him, I would not have been able to build any perspectives in my life.

Picture this: You meet someone for the first time in your life and you interact with him for the next ten hours and he leaves you with seven great principles! This was by far the most eccentric moment of my life! I had no clue that my life was about to turn into a conundrum after this!

FOCUS ON YOUR STRENGTHS RATHER THAN YOUR WEAKNESSES!

Mr. Raghuvendra Sanghvi (Professor, Historian & Philanthropist) began his speech with this remark. I had always heard everyone say that one should work on their weaknesses to succeed in life. So, what did Mr. Sanghvi mean by claiming the reverse to be true?

He then explained:

"Your life is like a camera. Focus on what is important and you will capture it perfectly. If you spend too much time working on your weaknesses, you will be average at best. It is always the light that shines not the darkness. Focus on your strengths and your weaknesses will become irrelevant!"

ALWAYS USE THE BOTTOM UP APPROACH

Always start with the end in mind. Define your goals first and then do a back calculation to understand your first step! So basically saying:

YOUR FIRST STEP IS TO DEFINE THE LAST STEP FIRST!

Here is an example:

Take a piece of white paper. Write down your aim at the bottom of the page and then keep going reverse. He then asked me for a piece of paper and started scribbling with his pen. I still have the original piece of paper that Mr. Sanghvi used to explain this phenomenon. Below is a snapshot for your reference:

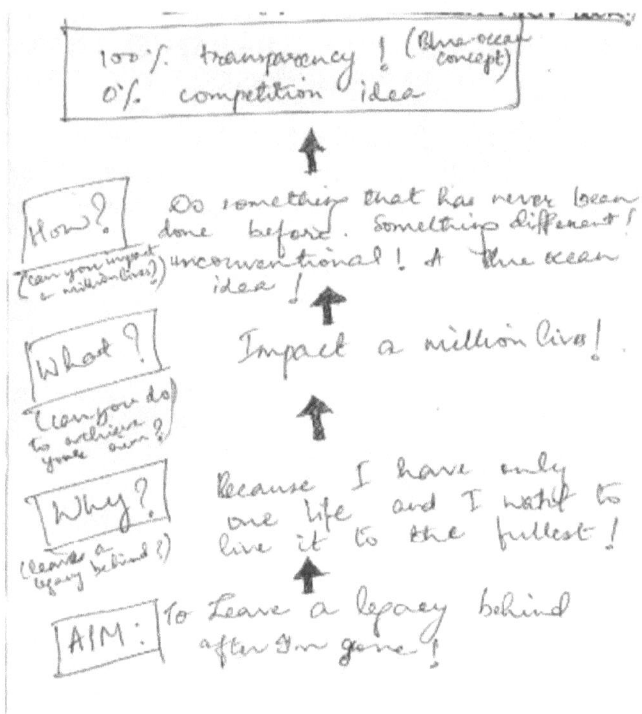

He then explained the blue ocean concept to me and how you can create a market space for yourself with zero competition, how innovation is incomplete without a transparent idea and how an unprecedented concept can become your life's greatest venture.

I repeated the same exercise after quitting my job and below was the result:

My Idea: The only formula in the world to write YOUR-FIRST-BOOK!

What is your blue-ocean idea?

TRUST IS THE GOLDEN ELEMENT THAT BINDS ALL HUMANS

"Money can come to you twice, but trust once lost can never be earned back!"

The biggest binder between you and your customer is trust. No business in this world can run without trust. The toughest thing about trust is that it's very difficult to build and very easy to destroy. The easiest and also the toughest way to impact a million lives is to make your customers trust you!

When I started my own business, I started with just one thought in my head: How can I build trust between my customer and me? The biggest reason why I have been able to work with thousands of people is because they trusted me and had faith in my business. If 'YOUR-FIRST-BOOK' is the world's most successful model today to writing your first book, then this has been possible only because I have never let them down and so they trusted me and passed it on to my next customer!

CURIOSITY IS YOUR BIGGEST BUSINESS, SO BID UPON IT

Mr. Sanghvi: "Did you know there is a philosophy around the world that claims that humans are from another planet? The only reason for that is that there is no other living being as close and as powerful as the human-being! This is a great divide in the history of evolution! Out of 500 billion species, how does only one species begin to dominate the planet?"

One and the only thing no one can ever steal from you is your power to be CURIOUS! Curiosity leads to creativity. When your CURIOSITY knows no boundaries, you begin to be CREATIVE!

"The world is dominated by only 1% of the people. Do you know why? This is because they are extremely curious. They do not stop questioning the status-quo! What makes them unconventional is their NEVER-ENDING CURIOSITY TO BUILD SOMETHING BETTER!"

THE POWER OF BEING HUMAN

Mr. Sanghvi then explained how humans enjoy seven distinct features that no other living being does.

- Erect posture

- High brain to body-weight ratio

- An opposable thumb

- Year-long reproductive cycle

- Pre-frontal cortex or the Neocortex in the brain/

- Rationality

- Speech

- Language

He explained how the erect posture enabled a man to strand straight and look far in the distance. This helped him to protect himself from predator animals. Unlike four-legged animals, man had the advantage of height and could use his two hands for other purposes whereas an animal used all four limbs for locomotion. He then explained the concept of Freeze-Fight-Flight and the development of the human brain. The power of the opposable thumb enabled man to use tools and protect himself. How most animals do not have a year-long reproductive cycle and so are becoming extinct unlike humans who enjoy a year-long reproductive cycle and so our population is ever-increasing.

The greatest advantage that we humans enjoy is the power to COMMUNICATE! Why is communication so important? We have speech to talk to other humans for carrying out our daily needs and speech is incomplete without language. The power of language helps us translate our thoughts into words. He then explained that communication is not fully understood yet.

George Bernard Shaw once said, "The single biggest problem with communication is the illusion that it has taken place."

He then talked about the human psychology and explained valence (Emotion, Pleasure, Suffering, Anger, and Fear). The reason why people don't connect with each other at the same level lies within the human brain and its understanding. The problem is that people have preconceived notions and so they don't connect with you at the same level. The only way to end this is to express your thoughts by telling them a story because people have no preconceived notions about a story!

He then talked about highly successful people and their biggest secret - the power to talk in stories and not in facts!

100% FOOL PROOF COMMUNICATION - TELL A STORY - DON'T TALK TOO MUCH FACTS - DATA AND NUMBERS WARD OFF PEOPLE - STORIES BIND THEM - MORE MACRO, GLOBAL AND STORY-ORIENTED!

Mr. Sanghvi taught me the science of connecting the dots through Convictions, Context, Comparison, Contrast and Culture. This is the POWER OF BEING HUMAN!

INEQUALITY IS INEVITABLE

Mr. Sanghvi: "Article 14 of the Indian constitution talks about the right to Equality for all citizens irrespective of their religion, cast, creed, sex, etc. But this is the biggest farce of the human race!"

I was flabbergasted!

He said that you need to go back in time to understand this phenomenon. Darwin's theory of the *Survival of the Fittest* clearly explains how evolution has wired living beings for natural selection or the preservation of preferred races in the struggle for life. This definitely means that inequality is the preferred form of nature!

Let's take a very basic example. Imagine a mason and the CEO of a company. If both were actually equal to society, there wouldn't be any difference between them. The biggest blasphemy then would be that no individual would ever strive to perform better, par excellence. No gadgets, no science, no technology, no form of art would have ever been invented!

EVOLUTION HAS WIRED OUR BRAINS TO BE INEQUAL. THIS IS THE DEFAULT CONDITION. NO LAW CAN EVER CHANGE THE LAW OF NATURE!

Do you still think you need to take drugs to be high on life?

Such mind-boggling, mind-numbing and mind-blowing ideas from a man in one day! I was so stunned by the end of this discussion that I was busy noting down points in my diary.

This had by far been the best day of my life! I had just had the most ecstatic encounter of my life without actually doing ecstasy!

I was so overjoyed that I completely forgot to thank him. My eyes were gleaming with so much energy that I was in my own zone for the next ten minutes when suddenly Mr. Sanghvi called:

"Sharmin! Sharmin! What happened to you? Where are you lost? And why are you smiling so much?"

"Nothing Sir. Did I miss something?"

"Yes, the most important thing…"

HEALTH IS YOUR GREATEST WEALTH

Imagine waking up one morning to this:

"You have ONLY 24 hours left to live! So, plan your day accordingly!"

What would you do if you just found out that today is your last day in this world? Can you go back in time and change the cycle of events? Will you be able to achieve all your dreams in the next 24 hours?

Of course not! You can't afford to keep waiting until things get worse. Money comes and goes, success and fame are a part of your life, but your health is the only one thing which is your biggest treasure. You can't afford to lose it!

I did not realise why he said the above until one day I got the news. Mr. Sanghvi passed away last year due to lung cancer. I could not even meet him for one last time to thank him for what he had taught me on that day. By the time I reached, his funeral had already taken place. Though he was gone, his principles are still etched on my mind forever and I shall pass it on to as many generations as possible.

III.
SUSPENSE

- What can anger do to you if put to constructive use?

What has been the most frustrating experience that you have ever had in your lifetime? Imagine being drunk to the core, incredibly high, unlimited volumes of erotic drama, your endo-cranial unit at the edge of smothering every glowing candle, an urge so loud and blaring that every window pane would break into pieces. Imagine being at the peak of your heightened pleasures when your partner or spouse just arrived before you could cum and then instead of reciprocating to you, turned over and fell asleep!

*Your Reaction: What the f*** just happened? Do something b****! (Irrespective of gender, no I'm not a female male chauvinist!)*

I have travelled to twenty-one states across India *(I probably know the street life better than any politician in this country and I might be able to produce multiple angles of the Indian society if I were to run the next Prime Ministerial elections)*, seen people run around every day to fulfil their daily chores and get back home only to eat the last meal of the day and go to sleep only with deep tensions about how to start the next day and how not to spend an extra penny the upcoming month. 80% of the country's youth wakes up every day only to curse the government, talk about all the existing problems in the society and go back to sleep not doing anything about it. Why is it that 99% of parents in India want their kids to become either a doctor or an engineer or a lawyer and then be placed with a multi- national company, earn big dough, buy a flat, a car and then get settled with a spouse chosen by his/her parents mostly and then mandatorily have two kids within the first four to five years of marriage? You see a car having met with an accident, a man bleeding to death literally and instead of calling the ambulance, all you do is just stand and wait until one benevolent soul comes and saves the poor man from breathing his last. You see an auto driver or a bus conductor misbehaving with a lady passenger and instead of protesting and yelling at the man for his rude demeanour, just stand and enjoy the lady getting ripped apart only because she doesn't know the local language. You work your brains out at the IT company writing codes, analysing data, cursing your boss, enabling high sales for your clients, projecting your company's growth by three times in the next quarter only to not get a share of that extended revenue and then go sprint with your hard-earned money at a nearby pub drinking all night, smoking piles of cigarettes to get high and again go back to that same office and repeat the entire cribbing process!

So, I thought of giving a name to this estranged group of people:

THE CONSTIPATED JUNTA!

Why constipated? Need I explain? Only constipation can lead to unwanted frustration causing more frustration to still not drink enough water to cure the constipation only to get further constipated. WOW!! Do you know the real reason for such insensitivity?

Lack of Perspectives!

Do you know the real reason for lack of perspectives?

Poor Parenting!

Yes, you heard it right! Now let me connect the dots and explain how:

When a child is born in a family, even before s/he can realise who their parents are, their future is already decided. Doctor/Engineer/Lawyer/Scientist…

Why?

Because our mentality is set: Risk Averse! Everything we do or wish to do should fetch us great returns. Do not invest your time in anything else. Be it investments or your life, each should have great returns so that you can rest assured. I call this the 'Need for Security' attitude. You should grow up to get a job at a firm, get married and have two kids at least.

Not one parent says:

"My son or daughter is going to build the next big thing and create a huge impact in this world!"

Imagine what could happen if every parent started thinking like this. If the first thing you heard every morning was to create impact, if after your daily school prayer, you had to take an 'Impact Oath' and after your last meal of the day, instead of bed time stories, your parents recited stories of great men and women and how they impacted the world and created a great human race. Can you imagine the power of such a childhood?

Unfortunately, our parents harbour this 'All Employees, No CEO' attitude which eventually forces every individual to flush away their lives just like their parents did. Why would any parent have a problem if their son or daughter were to start the next Facebook or Google or Apple?

Biggest contribution of poor parenting: Anger among the youth! When this anger crosses all heights, what the youth eventually falls prey to: Frustration! But what happens when this frustration is put to constructive use: Rebellion.

REBELLIOUS!

(1st pillar of the RACIST Hexagon)

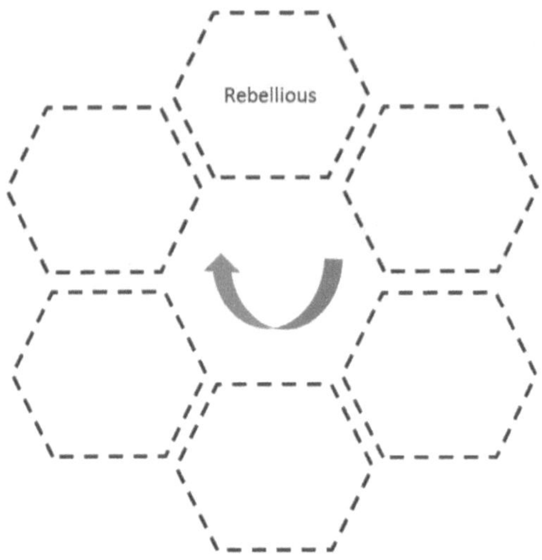

Do you know who the real father of Capitalism is? Charles Darwin. Now for all the believers of Capitalism and followers of Adam Smith: Father of Economics, I don't intend to hurt your beliefs or emotions in any way. But there is a strong rationale behind why I am saying so. You need to understand a bit about evolution to get a whole new perspective about Capitalism.

Coexistence theory is a framework to understand how competitor traits can maintain species diversity and stave- off competitive exclusion even among similar species living in similar environments. Coexistence theory explains the stable coexistence of species as an interaction between two opposing forces: fitness differences between species, which should drive the best-adapted species to exclude others within a particular ecological niche, and stabilizing mechanisms, which maintains diversity via niche differentiation. (Source: Wikipedia)

This was one of the theories that you must have come across in your school science lessons. The theory of coexistence was not accepted for various reasons. Darwin's theory of the survival of the fittest explains how one animal beats another in the process of natural selection. For an animal to survive, he needs to move up in the food chain. As a result, we are wired for competition due to the entire evolutionary process. If there were no competition, there would be no jealousy, there would be no curiosity, there would be no inventions, there would be no interest to outperform other species (other companies) and there would be no capitalism. Evolution has wired us humans to be capitalists. Unfortunately, some of us do not accept capitalism considering it to be selfish, shrewd and anti- social.

Just to put things into perspective, after the second world war, the world was divided into two sides, the Capitalists led by the United States of America and the Socialists led by the Union of Soviet Socialist Republics (U.S.S.R). The world was divided into a bipolar world as most of the countries aligned to one of these superpowers due to their security issues. This gave birth to a cold war situation which never really became hot as both the superpowers had nuclear deterrents against each other. Jawaharlal Nehru, the first Prime Minister of independent India conceived the Non-Aligned Movement (NAM) according to which a few countries (Egypt, Indonesia, Ghana, Yugoslavia) including India chose to not align to either of the superpowers. Now, you must have read in your Civic books that this was such a brave and noble decision been made by our first Prime Minister. But I would like to express my democratic rights and tell you that according to me this was the biggest mistake to have made for a nation that had just got independence after two hundred years of slavery. Had India chosen to align to the Capitalist world, we would not be considered a developing nation today. Our attitudes would not be corruption driven, we would not procrastinate and there would be more industries in India than agriculture. Ford, Toyota, Coca-Cola and other companies would have been born in India. Need I explain more?

But since India chose its own way, development had stagnated for a very long time. A developing nation has its own problems and these problems have their own consequences: People become more Aspirational!

ASPIRATIONAL!

(2nd pillar of the RACIST Hexagon)

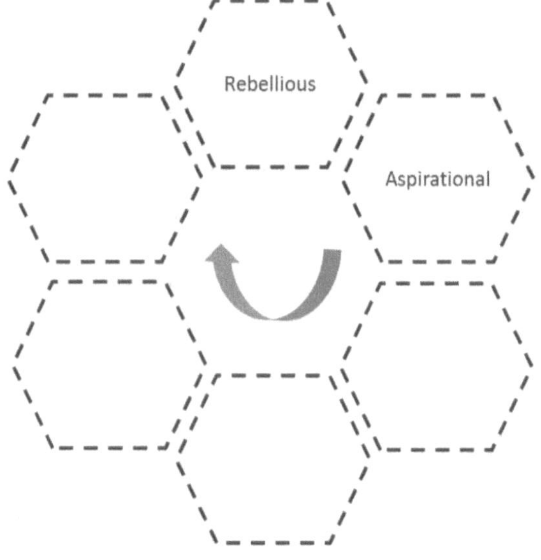

Have you ever seen a duck floating on water? Doesn't it look absolutely calm, as if it is completely undeterred by anything else? But if you look underneath the water, only then you would realise the great vigour that the duck paddles with below the surface to appear that calm above the surface. Have you heard about Gregor Johann Mendel, the botanist who is regarded as the father of genetics? You must have read about his famous experiment on the pea plant to define the laws for inheritance of traits in an organism. Let me give you a brief about his experiment. Mendel began a series of experiments on the pea plant (Pisum sativum) to study the pattern of inheritance of various characters. He chose pea plants for three reasons.

First, pea plants are self-pollinating. Second, they are easy to cultivate. Third, they have sharply defined characters.

Mendel chose to study seven different characters in pea plants. Each of these characters such as height, seed shape, seed colour, etc., had two sharply defined and contrasting traits (e.g., tallness and dwarfness, round seed and wrinkled seed, yellow seed and green seed).

He crossed a variety of pea plant carrying a particular trait (e.g., tallness) of a character (such as height) with another variety having a contrasting trait (e.g., dwarfness) of the same character. These two plants were considered as the parental generation (P). The generation that was produced by crossing these two was called the first filial generation (F1). When F1 plants were crossed among themselves, the generation that was produced was called the second filial generation (F2).

The results of Mendel's experiments showed the following:

1. Whenever two traits of a character were crossed, the F1 plants showed only one of the traits; the other trait never appeared. It did not matter whether the trait came from the pollen or the egg.

2. The trait that did not appear in F1 reappeared in F2, but in ¼ of the total number of plants.

Hence the term *gene* was coined that defined the factors responsible for the inheritance of traits and the rest is

Genetics. Let us not delve into great details for now. Now let me ask you a simple question: What do you think was the basis for the discovery of Genetics? The answer lies in one word: **Contrast**! Mendel tested on the pea plant because it had such strikingly contrasting features (height: tall and dwarf, seed shape: round and wrinkled, seed colour: green and yellow). The duck's appearance above and beneath the water are totally opposite of each other. Why do two opposite poles of a magnet attract each other? Again, an example of contrast! Why do some Bollywood films do exceedingly well than the rest? Yes, '***Bade-bade** deshon mein aisi **Choti-choti** baatein hoti rehti hain*'. Why do you want a BMW if you can happily own a Maruti which would take you the same distance at a cheaper price?

CONTRASTING!

(3rd pillar of the RACIST Hexagon)

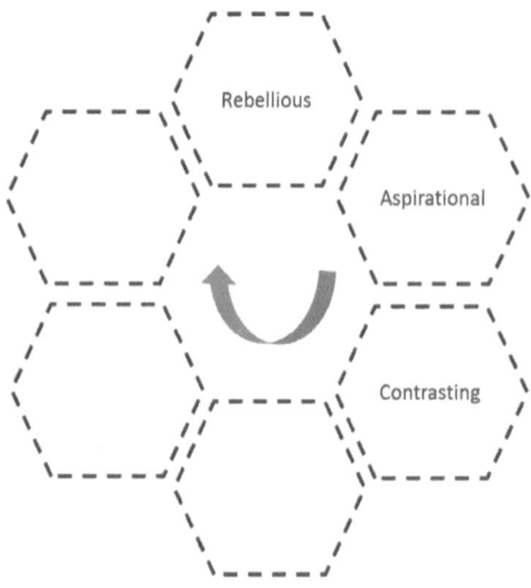

Do you know what is the most incompetent, procrastinating, discouraging, harrowing, and absolutely unworthy of brooding, concept in the world? The word: PERFECTION! The Ideal, a nonpareil, the crème de la crème, the ultimate, etc.: do such words really define a so-called 'perfect' world? I think PERFECTION is a term coined by an individual who was extremely lazy to do anything better. I mean how can an individual be perfect if nature itself is evolving every second. If in a room filled with people, you realise that you are the smartest in the lot, then you definitely are in the wrong place because then you have nothing more to learn, no more perspectives to gain. You are only killing your ambitions and encouraging a strange Utopian concept called Perfection. So just do yourself a favour and walk out immediately.

My life's greatest inspiration is in being IMPERFECT.

Did you know that the first guy I proposed to, said no to me? Why? Because according to him, strong- headed and ambitious women like me don't make good girlfriends or wives. *(P.S.: What I told him next would be a little out of context considering I enjoy a wide age group of readers!)* So, I was IMPERFECT according to him. As a result, I got rejected. I think being rejected makes you all the more stronger because you realise that the one who rejected you was actually never in your league!

Three advantages of being Imperfect:

a. Your thirst for doing something better never dies! You are not the promoter of Utopia, so you consider always getting there and you are never really satisfied. The reason for us humans being the strongest species is that our hunger for learning more is never really met by any means.

b. You are always criticised! The one and only gift that we all have bestowed upon us is that we love to criticise. I must say that I enjoy constructive criticism. It only means that the world is noticing you because you are impacting their lives or thoughts in some way or the other. For those who criticise only for fun, I tend to overlook and filter such clutter and jitter, because you get only one life and in this one life you can please only one person: YOURSELF! If you were to please a hundred other people you know, you would then have to be re-born a hundred more times, which again would be difficult for a lot of people to digest because you would then be disrupting not just the laws of nature but also a million lives for good. *(Just for the record: You can either hate me or love me, but you can't ignore me!)*

c. You are a free man! Imperfection frees you from all bondages, only the perfect woman or the perfect man has the fear of losing something s/ he possesses. If you already know that you are not perfect, there is no fear, nothing to lose and you are on a constant hunt for being better than your current state. Imperfection makes you Independent!

IMPERFECT

(4th pillar of the RACIST Hexagon)

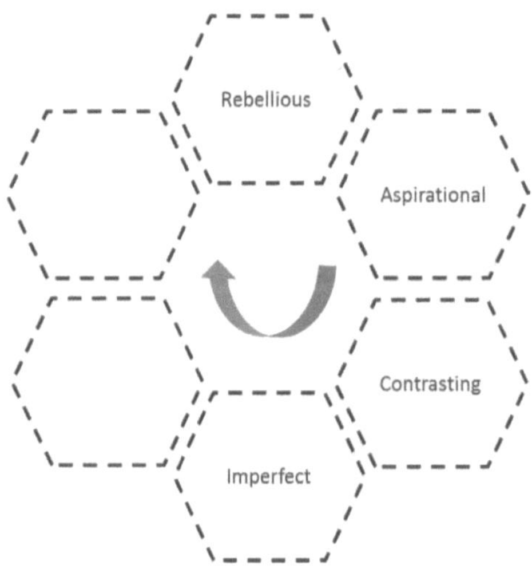

Have you ever heard about Abraham Maslow's hierarchy of needs? Below is the picture depicting the five different types of needs:

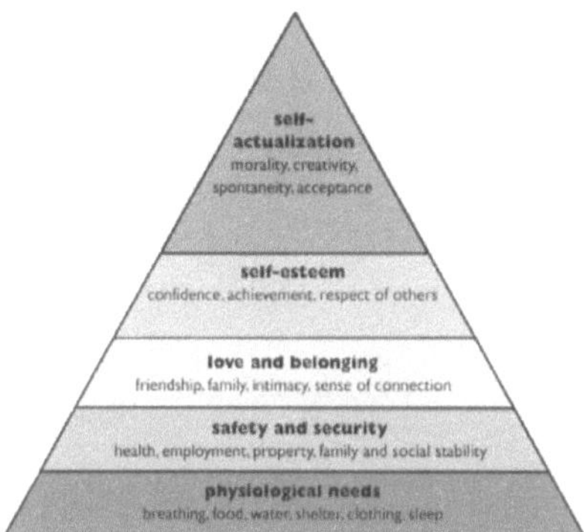

What, according to you, is the most important for you? How do you choose which one to go for and when? Hence, the term 'Priority' was coined. If you can prioritise your needs and focus on which one is essential, i.e., first things first, then you would notice a clear distinction in your living standards. Why do you think a few people become really successful very early in their lives? If you draw a Venn diagram to represent this, then the picture would look like as shown: Let Need be represented by N and Priority be represented by P, then Balance B is the intersection of N and P.

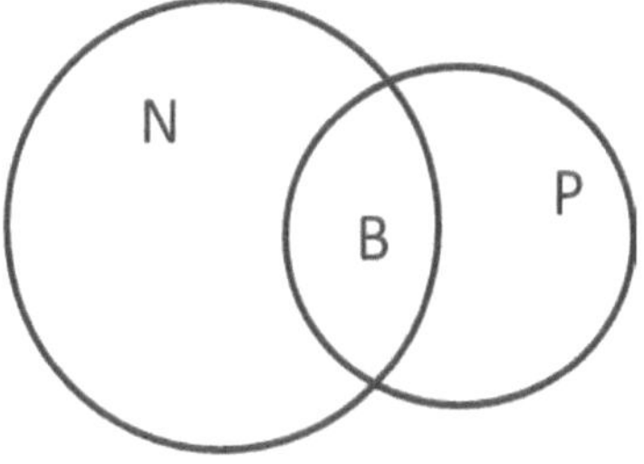

$$B = N \cap P$$

This is the balance that is the secret to having a sensational life like the select few in this world.

SENSATIONAL

(5th pillar of the RACIST Hexagon)

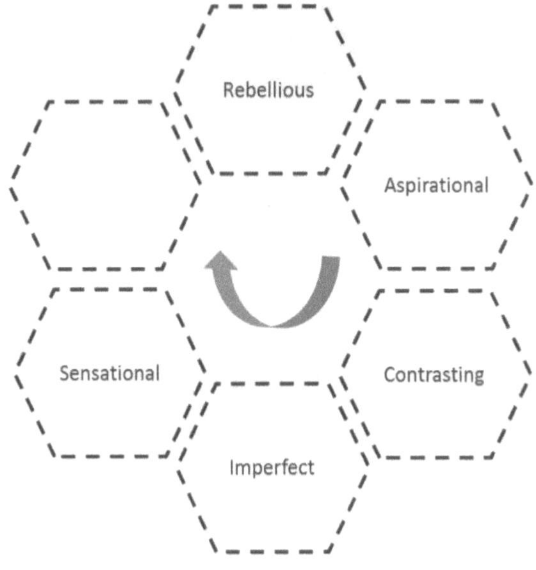

25 reasons why you should not be an entrepreneur!

1. You are on your own completely.

2. There are very high chances of your partner (boyfriend/girlfriend) ditching you.

3. You cannot get married and definitely not have kids if you have just started.

4. You always keep wishing you had a Godfather to help you sail through.

5. You have to be prepared to face all sorts of estranged questions from your investment committee: even if it has nothing to do with you or with your company plans. So, you always want to commit a crime: murder the one on the other side of the table!

6. Your mom will never stop convincing you on why you should stop and get back to a normal job.

7. You need to have exceptional levels of passion, oozing out at all times, both right and wrong.

8. You have to have incredible leadership qualities to both encourage and discourage people.

9. Even if you don't want to create an impact in the world and just want to make some quick bucks in a few years, you will definitely want to start the next e-commerce company!

10. You are the next engineer if you are planning to run a food start-up or an e-commerce company!

11. You don't need any formal education to run a start-up! All you need is to just START UP!

12. You would always hope to start-up in the USA: Investment ready and not Risk-Averse!

13. You suddenly become an Indian patriot: World's destination for capitalising on the concept of the age of convenience, thanks to the growing population.

14. You are the CEO: CHIEF-EVERYTHING-OFFICER.

15. You don't need an MBA in finance to determine your company's valuation.

16. You are sure to become the next Sheldon Cooper and there are high chances of you getting a hot girlfriend if you succeed!

17. ABC of your life: AGGRESSIVE,BREATHTAKI NG,CAPITALISTIC.

18. You need to fail to succeed.

19. You need to change your attitude from being an impulsive spender to being an impulsive miser, at least in the initial days of starting up.

20. You need to explain the meaning of the word start-up to at least ten of your relatives and then smile at their stupidity.

21. You have to face all the crabs-in-the-barrel and still move on.

22. You might have to resort to illegal (in India), anti-carcinogenic options to stay up and not succumb to the pressure.

23. You will start giving unnecessary *gyan* and become the next advisor at an investment firm if your company really takes off.

24. Your default poison: I love to drink BEER!

25. God save you if you are a woman entrepreneur and that too a sexy one!

However, if you still choose to be an entrepreneur like me then you definitely are:

THE HIGH-FLIER

(6th pillar of the RACIST Hexagon)

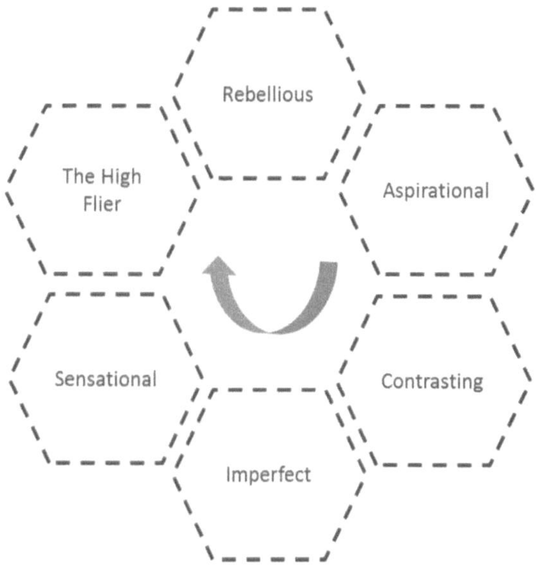

IV.
SUMMIT

- The Five Love Affairs of my Life!

THE ARTISTE YOU!

Have you ever experienced hysteria? Have you ever wanted to express yourself freely? Have you ever felt the urge to be heard? Now answer this: Have you ever performed on stage? Imagine a life of mundane responsibilities, working at office from 9 to 5 every day, taking orders from your boss and living a life that is a complete waste of time! Now imagine a life of eccentricity, excitement and extreme adrenaline rush! Which one would you choose? Would you want to get up in the morning to answer your office con-calls OR to do what you love to do?

This is exactly what I felt when I started the ART- RIGHT-IS Company! I wanted to live my life to the fullest, by not doing what others ask me to do, but by following my HEART. Arthritis is a disease caused by the inflammation of joints, especially in the knees due to insufficient nutrients in the body. But what happens when there is an outflow of energy, enthusiasm and extreme rush? YES!! We, at the ART-RIGHT-IS company make you weak in your knees! The ART-RIGHT-IS company is open to you only if you are not scared to let go and make your audience fall in their knees in surprise. We ENTHRALL, ENCHANT and ENSLAVE our audience, leaving them crave more and more!

On Facebook: https://www.facebook.com/pages/The Artrightis-Company/1497201567168580

I have been doing theatre for over 13 years now, but I started my own production house in 2013. Some of our best shows are listed below:

1. Potli Baba Ki Paltan

'Potli Baba Ki Paltan' was performed by a group of amateurs, experts and theatre enthusiasts. A combination of Gurus and Shishyas on stage, it was directed by both first-time and expert directors. The show was a camaraderie of talent, passion and desire on stage and encompassed a group of 10-minute sketches from various genres like comedy, drama, romance, tragedy, etc. The show was a house full of laughter riots, melodrama and male-female confrontations.

An Eccentric 'Potli' on stage

Bangalore Mirror Bureau | Apr 29, 2014 By: Vidya Iyengar

Potli Baba Ki Paltan takes a decidedly unusual approach to ordinary situations in people's lives, taking you through a gamut of emotions in different sketches.

Three babies talking about their experience in their mothers' wombs. A bride at a bar, on the day of her wedding. A rat murdering a cat or a doctor trying to prove you are insane. While you may dismiss these as impossible situations, Potli Baba Ki Paltan, an English play, will make you believe that these eccentric situations may as well be real.

Against a background of the adaptation of Mozart's Turkish March and Symphony, 19 amateurs and 6 experienced actors come together to enact eight different scenarios directed by six directors. However bizarre they may sound, there are several moments of truth, promise the production team. Details are picked up from day-to- day experiences and woven together, points out Sharmin Ali, founder of Art-Right-Is Company, which is organising the play.

The nitty-gritty of casting started in the month of November. Even so, the team has faced one big challenge-

-getting newcomers on par with veterans on one stage. But why this combination? According to Ali, there are many who want to be heard but don't get a chance. Also, it's easy, she says, to get experienced actors together on stage. But questions, "When will the others be heard?"

During the 90-minute session, you will be taken through four comic sketches, two rom-coms, one social drama and one tragic play. Ali says they believe in minimal props because the audience gets distracted by loud ones. "This is our style because we do not want the audience to get caught with the frills and lose out on the message," she explains.

The play looks at mundane situations from an unexpected different angle. Simple day-to-day situations, like that of a couple in a live-in relationship expecting their first child, are explored in the eight short sketches. The story of a husband plotting to eliminate the cat his wife is obsessed with through the rat, may seem anything but ordinary, but Ali believes, "somewhere along the way, the audience will connect with the characters, and feel that they have been in a similar situation."

With so many directors, was there a clash of ideas? "To be honest, there were," says Ali. However, knowing that such a situation would arise, the directors were auditioned first. Once they knew and understood the scripts, each of them chose the play that they would want to direct. It was only after that that they auditioned for actors, music directors and lighting directors.

Sharing some moments from the rehearsals, Sandeep Paranjape, one of the directors, recalls a recent practice session at Cubbon Park, where people had gathered to watch. "What was gratifying was that they got the emotions right. They laughed when it was expected and were serious when the situation was," he says. "With a number of young working professionals involved, there's been a lot of juggling around to do. Each of the groups rehearsed separately, after which the entire play was put together," he says.

Even with it being much of a balancing act, they hope that at the end of the play the audience goes through the same journey as those on stage. After all, the common thread between the sketches is emotions.

Gallery

2. Erebus – darkness personified

Imagine what would happen if there were only darkness in this world. Imagine the most explosive and the most aphrodisiac experience you've ever had. Have you ever seen

God? Do you wish to live your life in reverse order, 'Born Old and Die Young'? What kind of a woman catches your fantasy? Ever witnessed a ghost? Did you know being gay is the most masculine thing ever? Is sex really overrated? Is death really your final destination? Did you know that you could experience the maximum pleasure when all three hormones DOPAMINE, SEROTONIN & ADRENALINE

are released at the same time? Do you wish to be at the peak of your life? Imagine an orgasm that lasts for 70 minutes: SELF-INDULGING HEDONISM AND PARANOIA!

AGE NO BAR! SEX NO BAR! SIZE NO BAR!

7 actors + 7 shades = 70 minutes of Orgasm!

1 PRODUCTION TO GET YOUR JUICES FLOWING!

In the world of shadows

Darshana Ramdev | Deccan Chronicle

"I sometimes have a tendency to walk on the dark side," said JK Rowling once. Then again don't we all? Everybody has their secrets, fallen prey to jealousy and revenge. It's human nature. In Greek mythology, the primordial deity Erebus was the personification of darkness, he has been identified as one of the first five beings in existence, born of chaos.

This evening, the play Erebus will explore the dark side of humanity, through seven explosive monologues, each, in their own way, shedding the masks and facades that society compels us to keep in place. Conceptualised by Sharmin Ali and directed by Sandeep Paranjpe, this play definitely isn't for the faint hearted!

"We have seven monologues in all, three of them females and four males," said Sharmin. They deal with the ideas of lust, death, homosexuality and obsession. "You have a

woman who was formerly a nun, talking about her first sexual experience with a man," said Sharmin. In this monologue, the protagonist describes her frustration over growing up in a nunnery and being held back from her natural desires. "There is a woman who has left her husband. After a couple of bad experiences with men, she decides to find solace in women," said Sharmin. An old woman sits by her son's dead body with a bottle of whiskey, describing her ability to talk to ghosts and asking her son to return to her. A feminine gay man says he is the ultimate object of masculinity and describes his journey from loving gay men to hating them. A psychiatric patient falls in love with his shrink. "She writes a book on his case and becomes very famous. When she does, she has no time for this man, who decides to kill her," Sharmin explained.

All men contain within them a measure of madness, wrote Yann Martel in Life of Pi. The allure of Erebus lies in the fact that if we look deep within ourselves and do so honestly, we find vestiges of the greatest horrors we can imagine, lying there dormant, waiting to be awakened.

<u>Gallery</u>

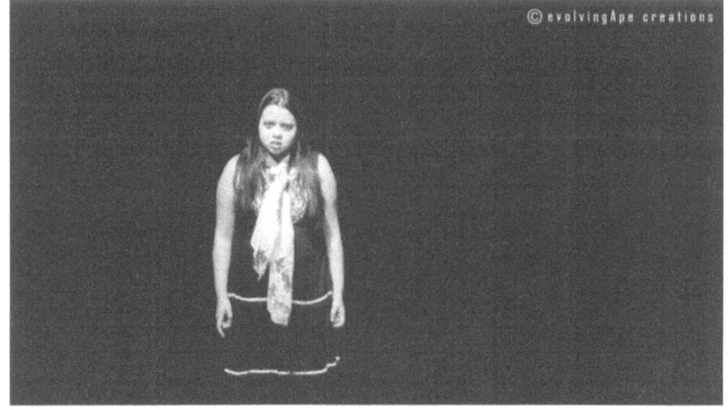

© evolvingApe creations

© evolvingApe creations

3. Auroras – the dawn

It was an evening to exalt your five senses with humour, delight, horror and pathos. Auroras was a collection of six short stories, woven together to dawn upon the human psyche. It encompassed six different aspects of human life: Evolution, love, friendship, health, shelter andcontemporary art. The scripts were selected to depict different layers of human life portraying human idiosyncrasies in different situations. Every common man can correlate with these episodes as they are a part of their lives. The ART-RIGHT-IS Company made another attempt at showcasing human emotions and societal issues through art and creative story-telling. The show comprised six short stories, each surrounding the above six aspects to give you an evening that you could cherish forever.

<u>Gallery</u>

4. The Penis Monologues: *'Use the force, but don't be forceful!'*

Ever heard a man talk about his deepest, darkest inhibitions on stage? Why are we so biased towards women and their innate controversies? Has the world been completely blind-folded that it overlooks a man's chapter? Why is the man always considered wrong at a divorce hearing? Is the man always wrong in a relationship? What does an old man at the age of 70 have to share with the world? How did Viagra become a blockbuster drug? How does a woman judge a man's virtue? Why are men the way they are? Does size really matter? Do you classify men as '3-6', '6-9', '9-12'?

For the very first time on an Indian platform, the Art-Right-Is Company proudly presented 'The Penis Monologues, written by the American playwright Jason Cassidy.

The Penis Monologues is a tribute to all the men in our society, to every father, son, brother, husband, spouse and that friend you look for when you are alone. Our society considers men wrong for literally everything in a relationship. The Art-Right-Is Company in association with Jason Cassidy presented the Penis Monologues to show the real picture of a man's life.

UNCUT – THE MALE RETORT!

Words of Wisdom from down there

By Vidya Iyengar, Bangalore Mirror Bureau | Aug 12, 2014

After the Vagina Monologues, men can have their say with this new play which puts them centre stage.

Have we reached a point where men are being suppressed in society? Are they typecast as the doer of wrongs? That's what Sharmin Ali, founder of the Art-Right-Is Company feels. Which is the reason, the woman director and producer is bringing Penis Monologues with the intention of presenting the "real picture" of a man's life.

Originally written by US-playwright Jason Cassidy, the play has been performed at the Edinburgh Festival 2011. Ali, who heard about the play through friends, contacted the playwright wanting to bring the performance to India. "Why do you think the Indian audience needs to see Penis Monologues," was Cassidy's first reaction to Ali's request, when she contacted him in May this year. "To him, the Indian audience was conservative and he assumed that with the number of rape cases, women are anyway overpowered by men and wouldn't get the play," Ali says. But she reasoned with him - "Why are we so biased towards women and their innate controversies? Why is the man always considered wrong at a divorce hearing? Is the man always wrong in a relationship?" He was then convinced about the need for staging such a play in India.

The hour-long performance where 18 actors deliver 22 monologues evokes a range of emotions. From a guy talking about his first gay encounter to an elderly man recalling how he had lost his virginity to his mother's friend and yet another person talking about his wife who cheated on him - the play has actors from the ages of 18 to 55. Ali, who has watched Vagina Monologues says that the only similarity between the play which has been "done over and over again", is that the characters talk about their deepest darkest inhibitions. "It was a sort of liberation for women at that time. But now it's time for men to speak out," she says.

The actors, mainly amateurs, were chosen based on a written test followed by an audition. The reason for that, Ali says, was just to ensure that the actors were comfortable talking about something so intimate. "Secondly, it's a monologue. The man has to be comfortable enough to have a conversation with the audience. We can't stick to the script line by line," she says. Spreading the word through social media, 60 applicants were shortlisted down to 30, who were then asked to come up with some bizarre situations that they had to enact.

While the initial plan was that Ali would direct the play, as the rehearsals began, three directors joined in, each directing the monologues. So, what has it been like for a woman to direct a group of men? "I came in with my own ideas, but the group has added to them. With three other male directors I've also seen things from their point of view," Ali says. But the original play has been adapted to an Indian context. "There were some references to American sitcoms and cities which we thought the local audience may not relate to," she adds. The lack of any props, apart from a single chair and central spotlight, is compensated by an intense script. While the play is sure to tickle the funny bone, beneath it, the play sends across a message loud and clear - women need to understand and respect a man's emotional needs.

And now the men talk back

By Chetana Divya Vasudev | The New Indian Express

Bangalorean Sharmin Ali is putting together a theatrical response to The Vagina Monologues

Bangalore: Nearly two decades after the The Vagina Monologues was first performed by Eve Ensler, it's still running strong, and India too has seen several performances.

As a response to it, to give expression to problems that men face, American playwright Jason Cassidy wrote the Penis Monologues. Directed by him, the play was performed at the Edinburgh Fringe a couple of years ago.

Now recontextualised for the Indian audience by engineering graduate Sharmin Ali and presented by her Koramangala-based theatre company Art-Right-Is, play will be staged for the first time in the country in about a month's time.

Talking about how she came across the play, the director says, "I heard about the Penis Monologues from my theatre contacts, so I got in touch with Jason via email and then we chatted too. He wanted to know why it should be performed in India. After he was convinced with my explanation, he agreed and gave me full freedom to make alterations since, he said, I know the Indian audience best."

According to her, although Cassidy's play was a response to the play that inspired a movement, this one too is for women.

*"The Vagina Monologues was for women to express themselves. The Penis Monologues is about the s**t that men go through. That women need to understand because most often whether it's a failed marriage or a woman who's physically hurt, it's the man who's blamed and people are generally more sympathetic towards the women. Even the law favours women."*

However, she doesn't believe that the audience for her production, opening at KH Kalasoudha on August 28, will be restricted to women.

"I want all the women to bring their husbands, boyfriends, friends along because they will be able to relate to what the actors talk about, be it the boy who shares how he fell in love with a much older woman (20 years elder to him) and believes that love has no barriers, the man who has raped and the trauma that stays with him the rest of his life, the problems of a boy who has just attained puberty and his recent first time experience, a man who wants to tell his mother he's gay. The play I feel will help improve communication between genders," adds Sharmin.

She tells that 60 people were auditioned before the 23 actors, who will perform for it, were selected. "It was tedious but also lots of fun," says the 25-year-old.

Jack of all trades

Jagran City Plus|12 September 2014 Krittika Sengupta

Meet Sharmin Ali, who has tried her hand in almost all art fields. She is an actor, producer, dancer and a writer too. Cityplus has a tete-a-tete with the energetic personality.

Who says you can't be a jack of all trades and a master of all? Meet Sharmin Ali who is a theatre artiste, producer and even owns a theatre company. Her first book 'YOU' was one of the best sellers of 2014 nominated by Oxford and she is also a contemporary dancer. But above all, she represents the young minds that have got immense potential to make a difference in society.

Sharmin has her roots in Bengal and was brought up in Ahmadabad. In her earlier days, Sharmin had to beat many odds like food, earthquake, and riots but over the time, it has made her strong, self-defensive and more compassionate towards her work. In her words, "Beating all the odds, a person who was too shy, introvert, underestimated by many is a speaker now and the stage has become my best friend over the years."

Sharmin completed her engineering from Vivesvaraya University in Electronics and Communication but her desire to traverse the entire world made her a totally different personality than what expected, revealed the young entrepreneur to Cityplus.

THEATER

Sharmin had been associated with theater for more than 12 years since her school days and slowly started taking part in street plays as well for other producers in the beginning of her career. In January 2013, she started a theater company of her own—art-right-is productions where she is not only the producer but even groom the budding talents.

Sharmin aspires to bridge the gap between common people and theater that is usually perceived to be only for elites. In simpler words, Sharmin wants to untangle the art of theater that will cater to a much bigger crowd. "Everyone is naturally an actor; theater is not a rocket science. Theater is a mirror to our daily lives, the emotions we go through where one needs to wear the shoes of a character," said Sharmin to Cityplus.

AS AN AUTHOR

It's just not all about writing a book when it comes to Sharmin but the young lady has also devised a secret mantra for how to write your first book and get it published what she calls as a speedy story writing wagon.

Apart from being an actor, entrepreneur and author, Sharmin has even taken up the noble job to conduct counselling sessions for aspiring authors on how to go about their first book. Sharmin has already started writing her second book and wishes to co-write a book with thousand other young authors by next year.

JUST BE YOURSELF

As far as solitude is concerned, Sharmin loves to indulge in charcoal painting and contemporary dancing when she is alone. Sharmin had never undergone any training for both but it was her sheer will power and spontaneity that paved her path of success in all the arenas she stepped in.

In her words, "To be successful, all you need is attitude more than aptitude and believe in yourself." An inspirer, a modifier but above all, Sharmin sets an exemplary example to many of the young talents for to make best use of their aptitudes to make a difference to the society.

ಗಂಡಸಿಗೆ ದನಿಯ ರೂಪ

ರಾಘವೇಂದ್ರ ಗುಡಿ

raghavendra.gudi@timesgroup.com

ಗಂಡಸು ಎಂಬುದು ಹೋರಾಟಗಳಿಗೆ, ಆಂದೋಲನಗಳಿಗೆ ಅಥವಾ ಯಾವುದೇ ಬದಲಾವಣೆಗೆ ಎಂದಿಗೂ ಸ್ಫೂರ್ತಿ ನೀಡುವಂತಹ ಪದವಲ್ಲ. ಇದೊಂದು ರೀತಿಯಲ್ಲಿ ಅಸ್ಪೃಶ್ಯ ಪದ. 'ಪುರುಷ' ಎಂಬ ಪದದೊಂದಿಗೆ 'ಪ್ರಧಾನ' ಆನುರೂಪವಾಗಿ ಸೇರಿಕೊಂಡು ಅನೇಕ ವಿರೋಧಗಳನ್ನು ಎದುರಿಸಿದೆ. ಇತಿಹಾಸದ ಕೆಲ ಘಟನೆಗಳು, ವರ್ತಮಾನದಲ್ಲಿಯೂ ಪ್ರತಿಫಲಿತವಾಗಿ, ಆದಕ್ಕೆ ಪೂರ್ವಗ್ರಹವೂ ಸೇರಿಕೊಂಡು ಅನೇಕ ಬಾರಿ 'ತೀವ್ರ ವಿರೋಧಕ್ಕಿಂತ' ವಿರೋಧಾಭಾಸಕ್ಕೆ ಹೆಚ್ಚು ಎಡೆಮಾಡಿಕೊಟ್ಟಿರುವಂತಹ ಪದವಿದು.

ಗಂಡಸು ಪರ, ಗಂಡೆಂದಿರ ಪರ ಎಂಬ ಪದ ಹೋರಾಟಕ್ಕಿಂತ ಹೆಚ್ಚಾಗಿ, ಮ್ಯಂಗಳ್ಕೆ ಎಡೆಮಾಡಿಕೊಡುವುದು ಬಹುಶಃ ಇದೇ ಕಾರಣಕ್ಕೆ ಇರಬೇಕು. ಇದರಲ್ಲಿ,

ಗೀಳಿನಲ್ಲಿ ಕೊಳಲಾಡುತ್ತಾನೆ. ಈ ಕೊಳಲಾಟಗಳನ್ನೆಲ್ಲ ಬದಿಗೆ ಸರಿಸಿ ತನ್ನ ಆಂತರ್ಯವನ್ನು, ತನ್ನೊಳಗೇ ಹುಗಿದು ಹಾಕಿರುವ 'ಡಾರ್ಕೆಸ್ಟ್ ಸೀಕ್ರೆಟ್'ಗಳನ್ನು ಬಿಚ್ಚಿಡುವ ಸಂದರ್ಭ ಬರುವುದು ತೀರ ಅಪರೂಪ. ತನ್ನ ಲೈಂಗಿಕ ಅನುಭವಗಳು, ಆವು ಬದುಕಿನ ಮೇಲೆ ಬೀರಿದ ಪರಿಣಾಮಗಳು, ಸ್ವೇಚಿನ ಚಿಂತೆಯಲ್ಲಿಯೋ ಸನಿಹ ಕಳೆದುಕೊಳ್ಳುವ ಹುಚ್ಚುತನ, ಆಪ್ತ ಸ್ನೇಹಿತೊರೊಂದಿಗೂ ಹಂಚಿಕೊಳ್ಳಲಿಕ್ಕೆ ಸಾಧ್ಯವಾಗದಂತಹ ಕ್ರಿಯೆಗಳು, ಲೈಂಗಿಕ ಕ್ರಿಯೆ ನಂತರ ಅಸುಖ ವಿಸುವ ಆನಿಯಂತ್ರಿತ,

ಮೊನೊಲಾಗ್ಸ್' ಎಂಬ ಸ್ಥಗತ ಬೆಂಗಳೂರಿನಲ್ಲಿ ರಂಗದ ವೆ ಶರುವ ಪ್ರಯತ್ನವನ್ನು ಆರ್ಟ್-। -ಈಸ್ ತಂಡ ಮಾಡಿದೆ. 'ಈ ಜ ಯಾವಾಗಲೂ 'ಗಂಡಸಿನ' ಕು ಜಾಣ ಕುರುಡನ್ನು ಏಕೆ ಪ್ರದರ್ಶಿಸುತ್ತ ಸಂಬಂಧಗಳಲ್ಲಿ ಯಾವಾಗ 'ಗಂಡಸೇ' ತಪ್ಪಿತಸ್ಥನೆ? ವೈಯ ಬ್ಯಾಕ್'ಬಸ್ಟರ್ ಔಷಧಿಯಾಗಿರುವ ಹೆ ಅನೇಕ ಪ್ರಶ್ನೆಗಳಿಗೆ ಉತ್ತರ ಹುಡು ಪ್ರಯತ್ನವನ್ನು ಇದು ಮಾಡು: ಈ ಸ್ಥಗತವನ್ನು ಚೇತನ ಆr ರಂಜಿತ್ ಭಡೆ ಹಾಗೂ ವಿನೋದ್ ನಿರ್ದೇಶಿಸಿ ರಂಗದ ವೆ ಪ್ರಯೋಗಿಸಿದ್ದಾರೆ.

ವಿವಿಧ ನಟರು ಹ ಶಂಶ್ರಷ್ಟರು ಭಾವ ಪ್ರ ಹಾಗೂ ಆಗತ್ಯಕ್ಕೆ ತಕ್ಕ ಆ ಅಭಿನಯ ಪ್ರದರ್ಶಿಸುತ ಮೆರುಗು ತಂದು ಕೊಡು

Review of The Penis Monologues appeared in the Kannada section of Times of India

http://www.vijaykarnatakaepaper.com/Details.aspx?id=16035&boxid=33251437

Gallery

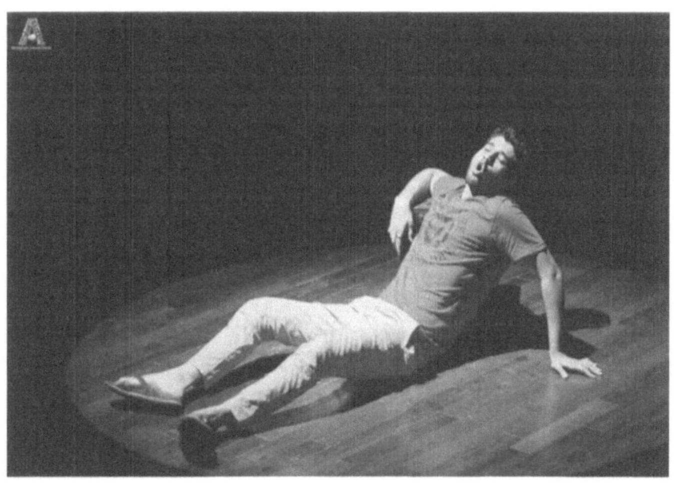

5. Chutzpah – *The Girl Store*

This has by far been the best play that I have written and produced in the last fourteen years of my theatrical experience. I need not mention more to capture your attention as I believe the below media references are enough to give you a good texture about the play.

Narratives of Power and Selfhood

New Indian Express, 15th April 2015

The city will soon catch Chutzpah, a story of seven women of varying age groups who share their journey into power and selfhood with the audience. This 90-minute musical satire is an original work written by Sharmin Ali. At a time when gender questions are being addressed more frequently, the play celebrates the latent power of all women. Says a spokesperson for the play, "One doesn't need to be a Benazir Bhutto or a Malala or a Kiran Bedi or an Ekta Kapoor. It is enough to let go off inhibitions and own your own power. The day a woman realizes her worth, no man or woman would ever be able to ill-treat her."

The play is performed by Annie George, Dimpy Fadhya, Shatarupa Bhattacharya, Sushma, Nakshatra, Divya Mohan, Harshitha Bhasker and Sharmin Ali herself. It is directed by Manoj Kumar Kalaivanan.

Says Sharmin, "My mother is a lawyer by profession, but quit practice soon after my sister was born. A very major aspect of my father's job required travelling around the country; hence we got the opportunity to stay all around India. My life seemed pretty normal until the incident that changed the course of my life forever. On February 28, 2002, in a Gujarati town, I woke up to the news of the Godhra episode. As a family, we traversed

25.7 kilometers of sheer misery and fear towards safety and away from rioting mobs. It was destiny perhaps because we had survived the earthquake in Gujarat as well."

This courage also saw her through episodes of stammering and also helped her find her calling in the arts. This play is her way of finding her voice, yet again.

Chutzpah will be staged on April 17 at Chowdiah Memorial Hall.

Chutzpah in Bangalore on 17th April

BY KAMAL PRUTHI - APRIL 7, 2015

Kamal Pruthi "in Gupshup" with Sharmin Ali, Bangalore based theatre producer, an actress, an author on her debut as a playwright with the play "Chutzpah" which is premiering on 17th April at Chowdiah Memorial Hall.

A brief intro on Chutzpah?

The play is titled 'Chutzpah' (pronounced as Hutzpah, a word in Hebrew). 'Chutzpah' refers to audacity, indignance and the power to do something unconventional. Each of the stories portrays that side of a woman where she has broken free of her inhibitions and defied the stereotype.

What was your motivation of writing this play?

After experiencing an unforgettable incident in Bangalore, I decided to stage a play to showcase some of the most influential women from our society. I shortlisted seven of these women and their stories and interweaved the seven stories into a full-length play.

Tell us in detail about that particular incident that shook you enough to jot down and finally produce a play?

On the 9th of February 2015, I encountered an incident that practically shook up the reason for my existence. I was travelling in an auto rickshaw, and was passing by one of the poshest areas in Bangalore when I suddenly saw a woman being brutally beaten up by an auto driver. What boggled my mind completely was that there were at least 30 people standing on the road and witnessing the incident and not one of them had the courage to intervene and help the lady.

I asked the auto driver to pull over, got down and ran to rescue the woman. I asked that auto rickshaw driver what the problem was. He yelled, "Who are you? Get lost!" I was flabbergasted! How dare he have the audacity to talk to me like that! I threatened to call the police to which he said he didn't care and that the cops are his friends. I started taking his photo on my phone and threatened to call the media and expose him. He suddenly fled. I turned to the woman. Her face was scratched all over and she was bleeding. I asked her what the issue was. She said the autowala owed her 30 rupees from the ride. When she asked him for the change, he refused to give it back to her and the argument sprang into an ugly fight.

I was very ashamed at what an appalling condition our society had fallen prey to. What if your mother or sister had been the victim here? Would you still be quiet?

Well, that's indeed shameful. Who is your source of inspiration for writing this piece?

Exactly a year before, I travelled to 15 states across India. I was extremely fortunate to have met hundreds of women with extraordinary stories. These women are neither famous nor rich and powerful enough, but their stories are so impactful that the world needs to know them! These women are from old-age homes, rehabilitation camps or orphanages and are considered unwanted by our so-called society. But each one of them epitomize womanhood. They are proof to the fact that women are wired to be the stronger gender by evolution.

Well this debate has been going on for ages, who in your opinion is a stronger gender?

If a woman can give birth to a child, she can practically achieve anything. Yes, a woman might be physically weaker to a man, but when it comes to emotional/mental decisions or bearing with a loss, history stands proof to the fact that a woman is way stronger. These women and their stories are an ode to womanhood. A woman's biggest enemy is a woman herself and not a man. Unless and until a woman doesn't have the authority to take her own decisions and exercise her own freedom, she cannot be empowered.

Who is the target audience for Chutzpah?

Well, the play is a tribute to all women. It spans an age group of 7 to 70 years. The play showcases certain intimate and controversial issues of a woman's life. It is essential that the audience be very respectful and acknowledging to the sacred issues of a woman's chapter. Since a child's mind would not be able to appreciate such idiosyncrasies, we recommend all parents' supervision and only adults above 16 years of age be witnessing the performance.

How do you think the audience's reaction to the play would be?

I would say that I have grown mentally to a very large extent over the last two years. My outlook towards theatre has immensely evolved. I've written a script after a very long time, so I am very sceptical about the audience's reaction towards the same. But considering the fact that it's an original story with all real-life incidents, I can guarantee that each one in the audience will definitely be able to connect with all the seven characters. Also, dance and music lovers would be in for a huge surprise with all original compositions.

How different is Chutzpah from your previous productions? After "Penis Monologues", which dealt with men's perspectives, is Chutzpah going to be a female response to that?

The biggest revelation about 'Chutzpah'is that it is about seven real, brave women and their audacious and bold stories. Penis monologues only catered to a particular gender, but Chutzpah celebrates not only womanhood but also life in general. No, Chutzpah is not the female answer to Penis monologues. Chutzpah talks a lot more than just sexual nuances of a woman's life. Chutzpah is an ode to womanhood!

World premiere of the play Chutzpah at the Chowdiah memorial hall is in Bangalore on the 17th of April 2015. Tickets are available at bookmyshow.com

That's called Chutzpah

Bangalore Mirror, April 11, 2015

What's in a name? A lot according to some who have taken offence to the name of a play – Chutzpah. The phrase popularised by the film Haider has drawn untoward attention for writer and producer Sharmin Ali who has been harried by calls from people who have threatened to stop the production. "They don't realise that the word is actually pronounced Hoo-tz-pah and means someone who has a lot of self-confidence and is audacious. It is the most apt name for the play which is about seven women who have had a tough life," she says. Like the characters of the play, she too has a lot of Chutzpah. She told the lost-brain-in-transit- caller to take a hike and that she will perform the play come what may on April 17 at Chowdiah Memorial hall. And if 'they' have a problem with that... well, it's their problem.

Some Chutzpah! Sharmin Ali takes on the right wingers

Deccan Chronicle Correspondent April 18, 2015

A group of right-wing activists took offence to the play's title, 'Chutzpah'

Bengaluru: Chutzpah, written by Bengaluru-based playwright Sharmin Ali was a huge hit with audiences on Friday night at Chowdaiah. However, the week has not been without its share of hurdles for the 26-year-old.

*"A group of right-wing activists took offence to the play's title, 'Chutzpah', a Hebrew word meaning audacity. They mis-pronounced it, taking it to mean a vulgar word in Hindi ch@@#**. They thought I was doing something illegitimate, that was against Indian culture," said Ali, after the performance on Friday.*

The word also gained recent notoriety when used liberally by Shahid Kapoor, playing the eponymous Haider in Vishal Bhardwaj's adaptation of Hamlet.

"They said they would destroy my career if I didn't listen to them," she said. "I told them I didn't care and that if they had a problem, to show up at the venue. I even offered them free tickets!" Sharmin also posted the issue on Facebook, which led to a number of responses – enough to subdue the protesters.

The play was staged on Friday night, after the group received a no objection certificate from the police. "I told the people who threatened me that they could come to the venue and ban me because I'm unstoppable!" Now that's what we call chutzpah!

SEVEN WOMEN TELL AUDACIOUS TALES

By Falah Faisal, Bangalore Mirror Bureau | Apr 16, 2015 Art-Right-Is' new play Chutzpah mixes linear narrative with shadow dancing for the first time in India. The title of this play might remind most people of the film Haider but Chutzpah's writer and producer, Sharmin Ali, says that's where the connection ends. Having previously successfully showcased Penis Monologues and Erebus, this is her most ambitious production which merges shadow dancing, where dancers perform behind a screen and are in sync with the actor's words, with the narrative of the play and has taken three months of hard work to put together. Chutzpah, which means audacious, tells the story of seven women ranging from the age group of 7 to 70. The stories, Ali says, she collected as part of her travels. "Last year, I travelled extensively with my team across the country and met hundreds of women ranging from prostitutes to nurses and dancers. All of them, I realised, were simple women who had impactful stories to tell," she says. Despite having their stories, it took an incident to prompt her to write the stories down. "On February 9th, I was passing through Koramangala, near Jyothi Nivas College, when I saw a middle-aged woman being beaten by an auto driver. I stopped and interfered, I discovered that he was beating her because she asked for her change back. This made me feel that I should tell all these stories that I had collected," Ali says. She chose seven that she felt were the most impactful. One of the stories is hers too, Ali reveals. "One time I got locked in a toilet and was stuck there for seven hours. The actor essays what I did while I was stuck inside." The director of the play Manoj Kumar Kalaivanan, who previously directed Eelam, a representation of Sri Lankan life during the insurgency, sat through extensive auditions to find actors who fit the age group. The cast includes seven- year-old Nakshatra to the 65-year-old Annie George. To add to the challenges of bringing out this play, a couple of weeks ago, Ali received threatening calls from right- wing activists who had an issue with the name of the play. But all that is sorted now, says Ali, who has got a No-Objection Certificate from the police. "If someone still has a problem with it, I'll give them a free ticket to come and watch the play," she says. Now, that's called chutzpah.

Chutzpah: An Ode to Womanhood!

Darshana Ramdev, Deccan Chronicle

Sharmin Ali was 17 years old when she picked up her first book – incidentally it was Ayn Rand's The Fountain Head. Up until then she had never read any book that wasn't part of her curriculum and had spent most of her childhood being the object of mockery among her peers, because of her stammer. "I spent my days crying in the bathroom," she said. Today at the age of 26, she has already written one book with another on the way, a number of plays and has her own theatre company. Her earlier productions- The Penis Monologues and Erebus are darkly intense and humorous in equal measure, with a healthy dose of what Sharmin has been best known for- irreverence!

With her latest production, Chutzpah, which she has written and produced, marks her comeback as a playwright after a five-year gap. Starring Annie George, Dimpy Fadhya, Shatarupa Bhattacharya, Sushma, Nakshatra, Divya Mohan, Harshitha Bhasker and Sharmin Ali, tells the stories of seven women from around the country, stories Sharmin says, "the world deserves to know".

These are not your feel good, rags-to-riches tales, the women are not exceedingly wealthy or literate of conforming to any stereotype of success that exists in our society. Instead you will see a woman from a brothel, a seven-year old from an orphanage, a seventeen-year old who was kidnapped and forced into prostitution and then thrown back out on the streets when she contracted HIV and a bus conductor "With a wonderful story to tell".

The play opens with a series of monologues after which the women come together. "We have original music and dancers as well." The dancers appear during the monologue to tell and enact the stories in a shadow play," Sharmin explained. "All of these women have been shattered by our society, but have managed to break the shackles."

This concept hits home with Sharmin, whose life is made up of doing mostly the same thing. She met all these women when she travelled across the country last year, in a three-month trip that took her in a circumference from Rajasthan to Calcutta.

"I was looking for material for my second book which is why the trip happened," Sharmin said.

"They fascinate me because if I hadn't spent crying my days as a child, I wouldn't have been able to do any of this. I'm very grateful to the prople who put me down."

<u>Gallery</u>

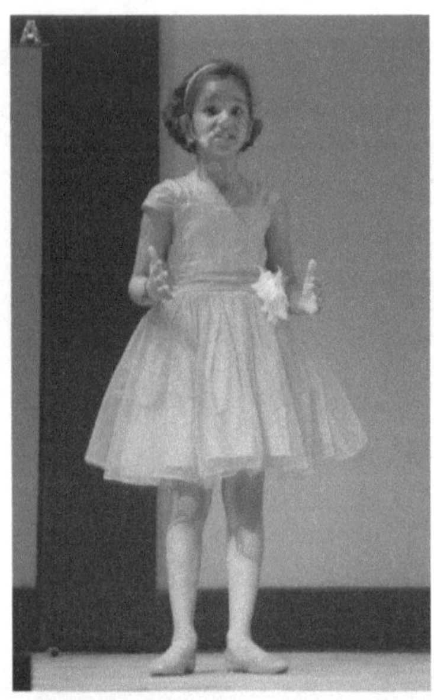

THE BLOGGER YOU!

This is a very beautiful and a free way to express yourself. I would like to share some of my blogs with you:

'10 Things You Didn't Know About Me: Sharmin Ali'

http://meetsharminali.tumblr.com/post/62230615710/1-im-not-patriotic-im-not-driven-by-any

1. *I'm not patriotic!*

   I'm not driven by any sentiments. I'm only driven by positive emotions, emotions that can constantly drive me to zag when the whole world zigs!

2. *I hate people who believe women's liberation is nothing more than BRA-BURNING!*

3. *I understood the meaning of LOVE at the age of 16: Losing a Virginity Early!*

   I realized pretty soon that I will not work for anybody. At the age of 16, I left home and went to a hostel in Delhi to pursue my higher studies. I quit my job at 24, and started my own company!

4. *People say start with a WHY! I would rather start with FOREPLAY!*

5. *Best results don't show up on search engines! They show on people's lives!*

6. *My Biggest Work Orgasms:*

   - *Quitting my well-paying corporate job at the age of 24!*

   - *Publishing my first book: Y.O.U ('You Own Urself'): http://sharminali.com*

- *Starting my own company, DIMENSIONS: http://dimensionalindia.com*

- *Starting my own production house: ART-RIGHT-IS*

- *Becoming a professional speaker and get paid for speaking!*

7. *I was blessed with a handicapped tongue! Yes, I had a terrible stammering problem!*

   I thank all the people who laughed at me, mocked at me, and believed I was good for nothing! It is because of their derisive behaviour that I'm successful today!

8. *I'm a staunch RACIST!*

   Rebellious-Aspirational-Contrasting-Imperfect-Sensational-The High-Flier!

9. *If I were to start motivational speaking, I would name my sessions: CALM-SUTRA!*

10. *You can either hate me or love me! But you can't ignore me! I'm IMPERFECT! Yes, and I feel proud about it! As Marilyn Monroe famously quotes: "Imperfection is beauty, Madness is Genius and it's better to be absolutely ridiculous than absolutely boring!"*

'It takes different kinds of people to make a world!'

http://indifference-to-society.blogspot.in/2013/04/indifference-to-society-is-not.html

INDIFFERENCE-TO-SOCIETY

Is not analogous to

INDIFFERENCE-TO-HUMANITY!!

Margaret Thatcher once said, "There is no society, there are individuals and their families..."

As I was getting back from work last night with a friend, riding on his bike, I suddenly spotted an old lady lying on the road, terribly wounded and bleeding on the roadside. My first reaction was that I hid behind my friend's back. But I soon recovered from the shock and got down. There were people surrounding the old lady trying to help her out. She wasn't responding though. Her white blouse was covered in red! Red, the colour of blood, anger, alarm, heat, love, and passion, it could have variegated synonyms. Here it was an 'Alarm'. I saw a young man, trying vigorously, calling up the ambulance for help, but the ambulance didn't turn up. I tried to stop a car-pooling vehicle to fetch help, but the driver simply refused. Another lady in a car said she could help, but since the driver didn't have a license, they would land up in trouble, hence another minute lost! Finally, an old man called an auto rickshaw to take her to the hospital. My friend paid for the rick driver and the rick left soon. I followed them to the hospital. It was just the old lady, the man who had hit her accidentally and me at that hospital. I asked the doctor if her condition was stable and if she would be fine. He looked perplexed. I asked if her bag had a phone number or an address to contact someone. The nurse had tried but no one responded. The doctor asked if I was responsible for the accident, to which I declined and said that I had come to see if she was fine. The doctor asked me to leave saying that since there was no one to claim her responsibility, she would be shifted to a government hospital. I was taken aback. What did he mean? Would he not treat her? When I emphasized him on treating her, he prompted, "Are you the one who's responsible for her condition? Why are you so concerned?" I was disgusted at the doctor's reply, his indifference towards the old lady. Luckily, the man who had accidentally hit her (and not willing to disclose the same) came forward and took charge of her treatment's expenditure.

Our busy schedules with our hectic timelines have enabled us a life of puppetry. We dance to others' tunes, and do not care for each-other. It's good to be indifferent towards the rules set by a harsh and fundamentalist society, but it's unfair to be not bothered about our fellow being. One should obliterate the wrong-doings of the society. I was crestfallen on seeing the attitude of the doctor towards an old lady. A doctor, being a life-saviour, should not be nonchalant towards his patient. When Margaret Thatcher made that statement, what she meant was, to not be dispirited by a pejorative group of the so-called society, which aims at setting up doctrines against the desires of any common man. By being unconcerned to the society, one should not draw himself away from the basic protocol of life, i.e., love and compassion.

I left soon after the man took responsibility for her condition. As I'm writing this blog, I pray that she is safe and would reach her home soon. Do not run away from an accident, help out the needy, as a small help at the right instance could save a life!

How to follow the THREE DIMENSIONS using your fourth one? http://theblogatdimensions.blogspot. in/2012/11/how-to-follow-three-dimensions-using.html

THE BLOG: DIMENSIONS

Why is it that we seek answers to some unanswerable questions? Why is the human mind out of our control? Why do we get attracted to people? And then why does that attraction suddenly disappear? Where do we go after we die? Why are we burnt or buried after we are dead? Why do some people fail to accept dominance or treachery? Why do some people always seek approval in life? Why do some people not follow where their hearts lead them to? Why do we suppress our anger when we know it is valid? Why do we not try to find a solution to a problem rather than running away from it? Why do we choose a career that is not our true calling? And the list is endless…

Someone steps out to follow his/her passion, and the criticism is far excessive than the encouragement. Is it not the time to have a different DIMENSION towards life?

We, at D.I.M.E.N.S.I.O.N.S do exactly what you need to get a different perspective, a different angle to your life. How do you enable yourself to be an entrepreneur, to start your own company? What does it take to be simply unconventional, to do what no one does, to find your true calling, to re-discover yourself?

WE WILL SHOW YOU HOW!!!!

How to get a different DIMENSION towards life? How to crack that one interview you had been preparing for? Why not become the CEO rather than an employee? Why not hire people rather than getting hired? How to follow the THREE DIMENSIONS using your fourth one?

WE, AT D.I.M.E.N.S.I.O.N.S WILL SHOW YOU HOW!!!!

Join us to be simply UNCONVENTIONAL, and get what it takes to be UNCONVENTIONAL!!!!

We are,

Diluted with Morphism, Enriched with Surplus Intelligence In Our Nature!!!!

Learn all about yourself, and the world around you. Quit that job and take the new step!!!!

We are VENOMOUS, SATIRICAL and SARDONIC!!!!

CHALLENGE US and ALSO GET CHALLENGED!!!!

We will show you the path to a new era:

To CREATE,

To DESTROY,

To MOCK AT,

To LIVE,

To KILL,

To ENJOY,

To LAUGH,

To DISPLAY,

To PORTRAY,

To FOLLOW,

To LEAD,

To THINK,

To BE PATIENT,

To BE RESTLESS,

To BE ADDICTIVE,

To BE CALM,

To CHANGE,

To PROVE,

To DISPROVE,

To MEASURE!!!!

D.I.M.E.N.S.I.O.N.S

(Diluted with Morphism, Enriched with Surplus
Intelligence in Our Nature)

Check Sharmin's blog

http://sharmin-ali.blogspot.in/2012/09/checksharminsblog-
inevitable-journey.html

"I have the choice of being constantly active and happy
or introspectively passive and sad. Or I can go mad by
ricocheting in between."

Why is it that some things can never be forgotten? Why do
people get stuck on just one point of view?

Why is it that we really need to pour our heart out to
someone? Some questions have no right answers...

Why is it that people get away with things so easily, when
you don't want them to? And, the bottom line is that when
you want something desperately, that is when the whole
world conspires against you…

Why is it that some people have to demand for their rights and some just get it for free?

Life's such a huge ocean full of questions. But the paradox of life says that learning the hard way makes you a better human being. This journey is full of so many rocks, that we have to choose the right one to be thrown apart, to reach ashore...

"Many choose to take the same path in life but only a few leave their impressions behind, others fade away with time..."

THE AUTHOR YOU!

'YOU' is a journey that encompasses four parts, from knowing about yourself to introspecting on the greatest beliefs of your life, from getting inspired by the 'blabbering junta' to realising your own secret destiny to freedom. 'YOU' talks about breaking the status quo and trespassing into a new world! It is road meant for each one of you suffering from a claustrophobic and nonchalant life that has led you astray. It's high time you realised that this is your life and 'You Own Urself'!

http://sharminali.com/

The Hindu
Writing her own destiny

Writing her own destiny

CHAT Sharmin Ali, who once struggled with a speech defect, shares her journey

PREETI ZACHARIAH

EASY CHARM, CARELESS CONFIDENCE: Sharmin Ali

> YOU WOULD NEVER THINK SOMEONE WHO HAD A STAMMER WOULD BECOME A PROFESSIONAL SPEAKER

Bangalore Mirror
Book launch
Edition: Bangalore   Date: 26/06/2013   Page no: 28   Clip size: H: 10 cm / W: 18 cm
TODAY
Book launch
Attend the launch of 'YOU: You Own Urself' by Sharmin Ali today. This is a holistic approach to self-empowerment and to discover one's unexplored potential. The book will be unveiled by Siva Arivaraj, Bollywood writer, director and producer. The author will be in conversation with Varun Agarwal, best-selling author of How I Braved Anu Aunty and Co-founded a Million Dollar Company.
WHERE: Oxford Bookstore, 1 MG Mall   WHEN: June 26, 6:30 pm   CALL: 9535328113

Bangalore Mirror
Happy birthday to... book!
Edition: Bangalore   Date: 01/07/2013   Page no: 2   Clip size: H: 10 cm / W: 14 cm
Happy birthday to... book!
This was one hell of an unusual book launch. When young author Sharmin Ali launched her book, Y.O.U/ You Own Yourself, on Thursday at the Oxford Bookstore, bookworms and others present at the store were a bit perplexed. 'Is it a book launch or a birthday party?' was what they were wondering. The air was cleared later. The diarist was told that the author was just too excited and was on an emotional high about her first book release and thought 'kuchh meetha ho jaye' was the best way to start... So the cake cutting. We wonder what old-school authors would have thought about this happy-happy-happy book birthday!

BESTSELLERS

Power Publishers new release: Y.O.U ("YOU OWN URSELF!") by Sharmin Ali

Y.O.U talks about how to own your life and transform it into an entrepreneurial hegemony. It defines empowerment with a four-step formula. A harmony of the visceral self with the nonchalant world.

PRLog - Jun. 23, 2013 - As a young author, Sharmin has presented a comradeship between life and business in her very first book. From the Newton's Laws of Science to a theatrical positioning of characters, from applying her engineering mind to a very subtle and holistic description of how to own your life, the author has featured her life in the form of a case study. A book that would come across as jolting, stark and incomparable, Y.O.U is a must read for all ages. The author provides an interesting depth into the human psyche through her book Y.O.U ("You Own Urself!"). A dedication to the 'claustrophobic' youth, the book traverses over four periods of time. From 'Knowing about Yourself' to 'Introspection', from making friends with 'The highly-segregated blabbering ones' to realizing one's own secret destiny to freedom, the author has beautifully crafted out a new generation of writing altogether. It is not just a book about overcoming your inhibitions, but a journey that every individual can associate with. The author portrays an aura of raw energy in her writing, influencing various aspects of life. From reckoning her biggest escapade as Charcoal painting to delivering each sketch with a story, the author sure has a very innovative bent of mind. For all those lost in their lives and the 9 to 5 corporate drones, it is advised that you grab a copy of this book and take the first step towards complete empowerment. Sharmin is the Founder at DIMENSIONS, a Consultant, an Entrepreneur, a Theatre Artiste, and now an Author.

This multi-talented, passionate and rebellious woman is on her way to make a difference in society. Sharmin has been quoted as saying, "I'm no perfectionist, but as Marilyn Monroe puts it, 'Imperfection is beauty, Madness is genius and it's better to be absolutely ridiculous than absolutely boring.'" To all those who suffer from a mental, physical or emotional handicap, 'Y.O.U' would teach them about how to dictate their lives and define their own rules against all odds because it is all about YOU, as YOU OWN URSELF!

THE SPEAKER YOU!

I had a speech defect all my life. Today I am a professional speaker!

What is the biggest contrast of your life?

I have got the opportunity to speak at many prestigious events like the TEDx, Millionaire Maker Seminar and the SAS Project. I have been invited to countless number of corporates to talk about my product 'YOUR-FIRST-BOOK' and about my book. This has been one of the most rewarding experiences of my life. Never in my dreams had I thought that I would be able to achieve the unimaginable some day!

https://www.youtube.com/watch?v=6kD7YedCM8s

Talk at the Millionaire Maker Seminar

https://www.youtube.com/watch?v=oe1v6Fy2TRA

Talk at SAS Project https://www.youtube.com/watch?v=OiArPslQWtU

Dimensions workshop

THE IMPACTFUL YOU!

Have you ever wanted to be famous? Have you ever wanted to create an impact on the lives of millions of people? Have you ever imagined writing a book?

Imagine getting interviewed by the number one news daily and journalists calling you up to schedule future appointments. Imagine the CEO of a Fortune 500 company inviting you to deliver a talk at their company's annual convention.

I will tell 'YOU' how to be a celebrity in your own rights!

I am the owner of a theatre production house, a Speaker and an Author!

WHY IS IT SO GOOD TO BE AN AUTHOR?

People take you 100 times more seriously if they know you as an author. Being an author has put me on a different pedestal of success altogether. I have at least 50 offers to reject every day! You will automatically be taken more seriously and you are a ready celeb! Writing a book has just not been about writing a book anymore. The way people talk to me is totally different. I know exactly how it works. I didn't know anything about writing. I was like you…… but I changed.

What goes into writing: **A structure!**

I wrote my first book in less than a week!

You can write and publish your first book in the next 90 days! I have a ready formula that I want you to take and become an author!

In a month, after having attended my workshop, people have shown such transformations, in a day they have written five pages and within a month, almost a novel. But my workshops are not for everyone! It is for only those people who are very serious about making it big in their lives as an author!

You are not fit to attend my workshop if you don't want it to be a bestseller! It is not about clapping at someone's book and admiring it!

IT IS ABOUT OWNING ONE!

I WILL TELL YOU HOW TO WRITE A WORLD-CLASS BOOK AND BE AN AUTHOR!

You don't need to be a 'JK Rowling' to write the next Harry Potter! What you need is my product **'YOUR-FIRST-BOOK'**, a ready formula to write your book and publish it within 90 days!

How it began for me: I always wanted to write a book but never really knew how to write in such a way that it would create an impact on my reader's brain. I would always write and then tear the page, thinking it wasn't good enough. What I REALLY wanted to know was:

THAT SECRET INGREDIENT TO WRITING A BESTSELLING BOOK!

I had been a non-reader all my life. All that I had read was my curriculum-based book! NONE OF MY ENGLISH LITERATURE BOOKS TAUGHT ME THE SECRET TO WRITING A BESTSELLING BOOK! SUCH A WASTE OF TIME IT WAS!!!!!

I was so disillusioned that I decided to hear it from the horse's mouth! So, I started reading a lot of bestselling books to understand what it takes exactly to **CREATE A MASTERPIECE!**

I had read almost fifty books and after having read so many of them, I could actually predict the story line of the fifty-first! I could connect the dots and understand why exactly a character was behaving the way he was made to behave. Why did a particular scene unfold in the middle and not in the end OR Why was a character removed from the story OR Why did the victim's mother not reveal the truth until the end?

EUREKA! EUREKA! EUREKA!

I then founded my own story-writing formula and named it **'YOUR-FIRST-BOOK'**! Using this formula, I then wrote my first book in less than a week!

Now you might be wondering that all this is BS! Is this really possible? Using a formula to write a book! BS! BS! BS!

Well, I'm here to answer all your questions and prove it to you that using my formula you can **CREATE YOUR OWN MASTERPIECE! SO, LET'S START THE WAY I STARTED!**

Short cut to a story

The Hindu | Feb 21, 2014

Preeti Zachariah

Chat Sharmin Ali believes that 90 days is all it takes to write a book

She wrote her first book in less than a week and now wants to help other budding novelists do the same. Meet debut novelist, entrepreneur, public speaker, blogger, theatre artist and motivational speaker, Sharmin Ali whose debut novel Y.O.U (You Own Yourself) reflects the author's determination to bring about a positive change in the lives her readers.

Yet this has not come easily to this multi-faceted, self-possessed young woman who believes in doing things differently, "I had a stammering problem as a child," she admits adding that the first person whose life she transformed was herself.

An engineer by profession, Sharmin worked in the corporate field for several years before quitting doing theatre.

She went on to co-found a production house, Plain Ice Productions and then decided to write. "I've always wanted to write but didn't know how to put my ideas across. So, I started reading a lot of best-sellers and understanding why they worked. After reading 10 of them, I realized I could predict how the eleventh would work. That made it easier for me to write my own and I went ahead and wrote my first non-fiction book is less than a week," she says.

Her experience with writing her own book made her realize that there was a need to share it with other budding writers, "There are so many out there and I wanted to create something that would make it easier for them," she says.

This has led to the creation of her latest product Your-First-Book.com, a formula on how to become a published author in less than 90 days. The CD of the program was launched at the Oxford Bookstore earlier this month.

The product hand holds a budding writer through the journey of writing and includes tips on how to start, how to position yourself, what to write about and how to get published,

"I've used the seven principles of Brain Science while creating this product. This will help you create your Magnum opus," she says adding, "At the end of the day, it is attitude and not aptitude that matters. You need to just get up and start doing things."

Three questions that will dawn upon you are:

1. Why should you write a book?

2. What should you write about?

3. How should you write a book and publish?

WHY SHOULD YOU WRITE A BOOK?

Six major reasons why you should write a book are as mentioned below:

- GIVE A **MESSAGE!**

- LET PEOPLE BE **AWAY FROM THEIR WORLD/SITUATION!**

- TO SHARE YOUR **OWN STORY WITH THE WORLD!**

- TO MAKE SURE YOU **LEAVE A LEGACY!**

- OFFSHOOTS: **MONEY, FAME, LIFE-LONG HOLIDAY!** AND THE MOST IMPORTANT REASON BEING

- WHAT LISTENING TO A STORY DOES TO YOUR **BRAIN?**

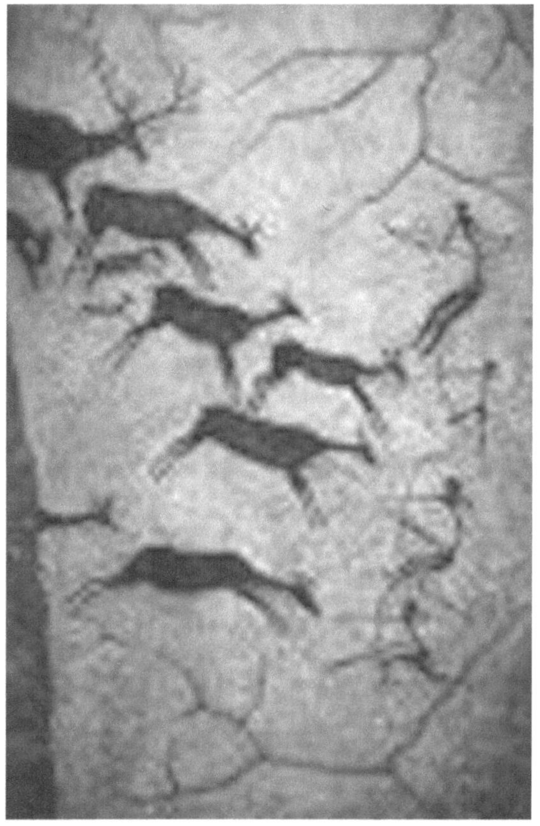

What does this picture tell you?

YES, it is a cave painting, available freely on the internet and is one of the most commonly shown pictures around the world!

> **For over 27,000 years, since the first cave paintings were discovered, telling stories has been one of our most fundamental communication methods!**

We all love stories, whether from a novel, a movie or simply a narrative. So, what exactly happens to the brain when you listen to a story?

If you listen to a PowerPoint presentation with boring bullet points, only a certain part of your brain gets activated called the Broca's area and the Wernicke's area. It basically hits our language processing parts in the brain, where we decode words into meaning. And that's it, nothing else happens.

On the other hand, when we listen to a story, there is a dramatic change in the brain activities. Not only are the language processing parts in our brain activated, but any other area in our brain that we would use when experiencing the events of the story also get activated.

If someone tells us about how delicious certain foods were, our sensory cortex lights up, if it's about motion, our motor cortex gets active. Now read the below lines:

- Sarah has silky-smooth skin.

- The dancer had wavy moves.

- Jim fell down the hill.

- I burnt the cake by mistake.

- Julia grasped the falling fan.

YOUR BRAIN REACTS TO WHAT YOU READ AND ACTIVATES THAT PARTICULAR CORTEX FOR YOU TO ANALYSE THE SITUATION!

A story can put your whole brain to work.

When you tell stories to others that have really helped you shape your thinking and way of life, you can have the same effect on them too.

> **By simply telling a story, you can plant ideas, thoughts and emotions into your listeners' brains.**

Good to Know:

The process of identifying the parts of the brain that are involved in language began in 1861, when Paul Broca, a French neurosurgeon, examined the brain of a recently deceased patient who had had an unusual disorder. Though he had been able to understand spoken language and did not have any motor impairments of the mouth or tongue that might have affected his ability to speak, he could neither speak a complete sentence nor express his thoughts in writing. The only articulate sound he could make was the syllable "tan", which had come to be used as his name.

Paul Broca

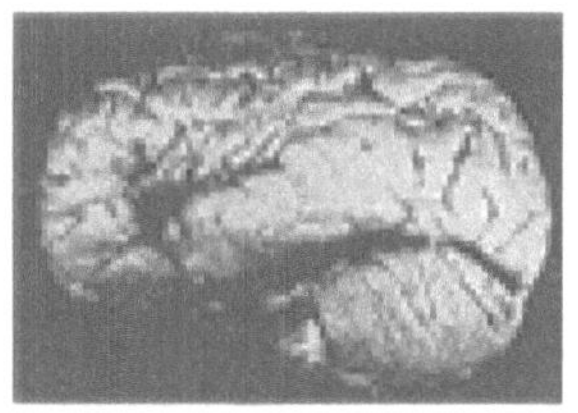

Tan's brain

When Broca autopsied Tan's brain, he found a sizable lesion in the left inferior frontal cortex. Subsequently, Broca studied eight other patients, all of whom had similar language deficits along with lesions in their left frontal hemisphere. This led him to make his famous statement that "we speak with the left hemisphere" and to identify, for the first time, the existence of a "language centre" in the posterior portion of the frontal lobe of this hemisphere. Now known as **Broca's area**, *this was in fact the first area of the brain to be associated with a specific function—in this case, language. Ten years later, Carl Wernicke, a German neurologist, discovered another part of the brain, this one involved in understanding language, in the posterior portion of the left temporal lobe. People who had a lesion at this location could speak, but their speech was often incoherent and made no sense.*

Carl Wernicke

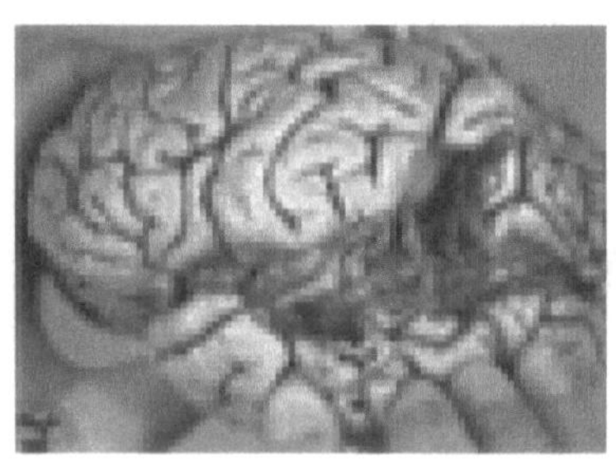

Brain with a lesion

Difference between Wernicke's area and Broca's area:

What is Broca's area?

It is the motor speech area.

Motor? Yeah, it helps in movements required to produce speech.

What is Wernicke's area?

It is the sensory speech area.

Sensory? Yes, it helps you understand speech.

It also helps in usage of correct words to express our thoughts.

> **Evolution has wired our brains for stories! There is no better way to connect with people than by telling them a story! So, make use of it!**

For those of you who haven't yet written a book, I want to ask you one question:

Why haven't you still written a book?

My team of experts did a survey and we found the below ten reasons as the major deterrents that stop you from writing:

1. **Lack of proper tools to write (Typewriter/Pen/ Microsoft Word):** As per our survey, we found the below results.

Tools used	Percentage of people (Preference of tool)
Typewriter	30%
Pen	65%
Microsoft Word	5%

Point to note: **It's not the tools that make the writer! It's the act of writing!**

2. **How do I begin?** I believe that you should start with something that can easily grab your reader's attention! Make it sound as horrible, as controversial and as bold as possible! **Because we love to get shocked! The**

more shocking the first sentence, more is the desire to read further!

3. **Fear of terrible reviews!** You should not write a book with the intention of getting a five-star review. The only intention should be to create an impact on your reader. Everything else is a deterrent.

4. **The right age to write (I'm too young or I'm too old)** EL James wrote the Fifty Shades of Grey at 40. It is now a major motion picture! Do you really think age is a factor?

5. **Fear of a Writer's Block! (I will never finish!)** As I have already said before, always start with the end in mind and use the bottom-up approach. You shall definitely achieve your goal!

6. **Fear of family/friends at the usage of offensive language.** If you try to please everyone, you shall end up displeasing everyone. You need to define the BRAND YOU and stick on with it.

7. **I have no time! (Lack of time management skills)** This is by far the most common problem. Well, even an MBA degree does not teach you to manage your time. If you really want to write and publish, all you need is to just start writing!

8. **Minimum number of pages or word count required to publish a book!** My first book had around 85 pages. A coffee table book might have only 30 pages. The number of pages or the word count does not define the author. Instead, the content is what defines the author!

9. **Fear of getting rejected and never being able to publish!** I was rejected by 16.5 publishers when I had written my first book! I finally rejected the 17th one

because they were taking too long to get back to me. Frankly speaking, with the age of self- publishing, this fear is now completely outdated.

10. **My story is no different than yours!** You cannot re-invent the wheel! You can only make it better! Positioning, packaging and parcelling are what matter rather than whose story it is.

WHAT SHOULD YOU WRITE ABOUT?

After an extensive research, we have found the below areas of interest that a majority of people have expressed. Which one is yours?

<u>Fiction Genre List</u>

- Action and Adventure,
- Chick Lit,
- Children's,
- Commercial Fiction,
- Contemporary,
- Crime,
- Erotica,
- Family Saga,
- Fantasy,
- Dark Fantasy (probably still a major sub-genre!)
- Gay and Lesbian,
- General Fiction,
- Graphic Novels,
- Historical Fiction,
- Horror,
- Humour,
- Literary Fiction,

- Military and Espionage,
- Multicultural,
- Mystery,
- Offbeat or Quirky,
- Picture Books,
- Religious and Inspirational,
- Romance,
- Science Fiction,
- Short Story Collections,
- Thrillers and Suspense,
- Western,
- Women's Fiction,
- Young Adult.

Non-Fiction Genre List

- Art & Photography,
- Biography & Memoirs,
- Business & Finance,
- Celebrity & Pop Culture,
- Music, Film & Entertainment,
- Cookbooks,
- Cultural/Social Issues,
- Current Affairs & Politics,
- Food & Lifestyle,
- Gardening,
- Gay & Lesbian,
- General Non-Fiction,
- History & Military,
- Home Decorating & Design,
- How To,
- Humour & Gift Books,
- Journalism,
- Juvenile,

- Medical, Health & Fitness,
- Multicultural,
- Narrative,
- Nature & Ecology,
- Parenting,
- Pets,
- Psychology,
- Reference,
- Relationship & Dating,
- Religion & Spirituality,
- Science & Technology,
- Self-Help,
- Sports,
- Travel,
- True Adventure & True Crime,
- Women's Issues.

If you still haven't picked one for yourself, please feel free to contact me through my websites and I shall get in touch with you and conduct an hour-long session **(ABSOLUTELY FREE OF COST!!!)** to determine your **UNIQUE AREA OF INTEREST** and define **THE BRAND YOU!**

HOW SHOULD YOU WRITE A BOOK AND PUBLISH?

I run the most blasphemous, the most outrageous and the boldest course ever:

"YOUR-FIRST-BOOK"

A proven formula to write and publish your first book in less than 90 days!

I wrote my first book in less than a week!

My biggest challenge to you is to write your first book in the next 90 days!!!!!

I want to share my secret formula with you and create your masterpiece!

Can you look at this picture and create a story out of it?

What if I were to give you the below words?

Ancient Civilization, Animals, Art, Background, Brown, Cave, Cave Painting, Chronicle, Communication, Conservation, Creativity, Depicting, Design, Detailed, Drawing, Etched, Etching, Fundamental, Heritage, History, Horizontal, Landmark, Message, Old Fashioned, Pattern, People, Preservation, Primitive, Rudimentary,

Shape, Sight, Simple, Symbol, Tour, Tourism, Tourist Attraction

Now can you create a story out of it?

My product 'YOUR-FIRST-BOOK' consists of the following four primary steps:

1. Great Writing Skills

    o The Content Creator Machine™

2. Engage & Entertain Your Reader

    o The Story Clock™

3. Structure Your Content

    o Finesse-Five Formula™

4. Publish & Sell

    o S.E.L.L. Your Book™

The Content Creator Machine™

12 C's Model™

This model consists of twelve C's essential to build your manuscript. Why is good content so important? Four purposes of your content:

<u>**Foreplay**</u>

➢ Initiate & Play

- Don't immediately go for the **hotspots.**

- **Take your time** before undressing your character.

- Once you do undress her, remember to **make it an experience.**

- **Light and gentle** wins out over **rough and fast.**

- Compliment and talk dirty in **equal proportions.** Show both the **strengths and weaknesses** of your character.

- Don't spend too much time in one spot, **keep it moving, else the reader wards off!**

- **Take control.**

- **Go downtown.**

- Make sure that your character is well lubricated before you finish up your foreplay and move on to sex!

- If she starts to lose the mood while you are in the middle of sex, return to foreplay for a minute or two to get her back in the mood.

**NOW GIVE YOUR CHARACTERS AND STORY
THE SAME EXPERIENCE!**

<u>Intercourse</u>

- 'You know that feeling like you're going over a hill and you get that swoosh feeling in your stomach? Your reader has to feel that in her stomach!'

- 'You know that feeling you get in your chest when you drink something warm on a cold day? Your reader has to feel that in her chest.'

- 'It's the feeling of wanting to be filled so badly that it hurts, make your reader feel that incompleteness that she would crave reading further.'

<u>Orgasm</u>

- This is where the reader reaches the climax, should be the most exhilarating experience in the world.

- Orgasm (from Greek 'orgasmos', meaning excitement, swelling, also sexual climax) is the sudden discharge of accumulated sexual tension during the sexual response cycle.

YOUR READER SHOULD BE ABLE TO RELEASE THE SAME TENSION AND FEEL SATISFIED!

<u>Afterglow</u>

- The pleasant feeling after sexual intercourse

- Your reader should bask in the glory of your masterpiece!

LET THE SENSE OF FULFILMENT LINGER IN YOUR READER'S MIND FOREVER!

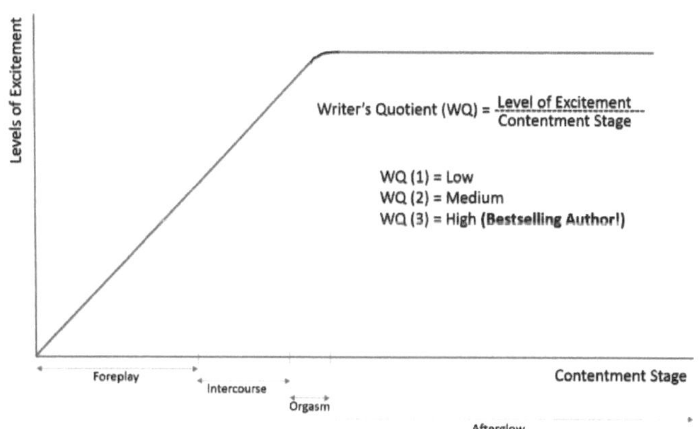

THE STORY CLOCK™

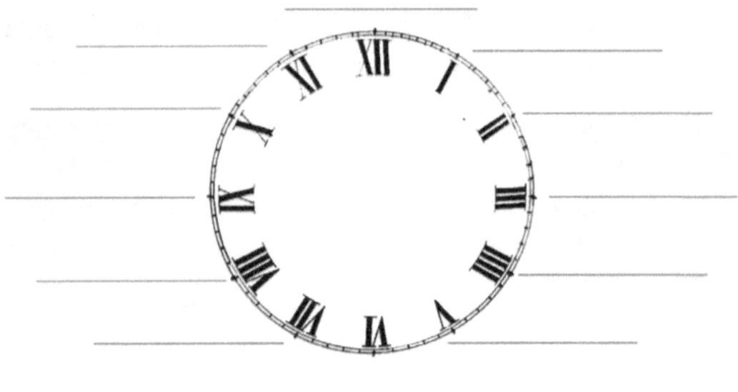

Each of the blank represents an important aspect to build your story. The twelve numbers of the clock are the twelve steps to building the perfect manuscript.

FINESSE-FIVE FORMULATM

1. __________ your piece

2. __________ your content

3. __________ your perspective

4. __________ an excellent material

5. __________your take-away message

Once your manuscript is ready, it is important to structure your content to convert it into a book. This five-step formula helps you to remove unnecessary and extra content and transform it into a readable format.

PUBLISH AND S.E.L.L.TM

Ask yourself three basic questions:

1. You have got your manuscript. Now, what next? How do you get it published and transform it into a book?

2. How do you make your book sell?

3. How do you become a bestselling author?

The best formula here is:

S.E.L.L.™

1. S __________ : How do you get a publisher?

2. E __________ : How do you engage your reader?

3. L __________ : How to attract your publisher into getting you boarded? Four fantastic ways to attract your publisher: **THE FANTASTIC FOUR FORMULAE!**

4. L __________ : Ten incredible ways to market your book!

GET THE MARKETING RIGHT!

The most important aspect of being a bestselling author is to get the positioning and marketing right. Why should a reader purchase your book? What is it that differentiates you from a million other authors? What is so unique about your manuscript that differentiates if from a million other manuscripts submitted every year? Let me put things into perspective through the following print ads:

This controversial print advertisement was created by renowned advertising agency Ogilvy & Mather. Altering an iconic photo into something entirely different captured the tag line "The Best Finish You Can Imagine" in an entirely unexpected fashion.

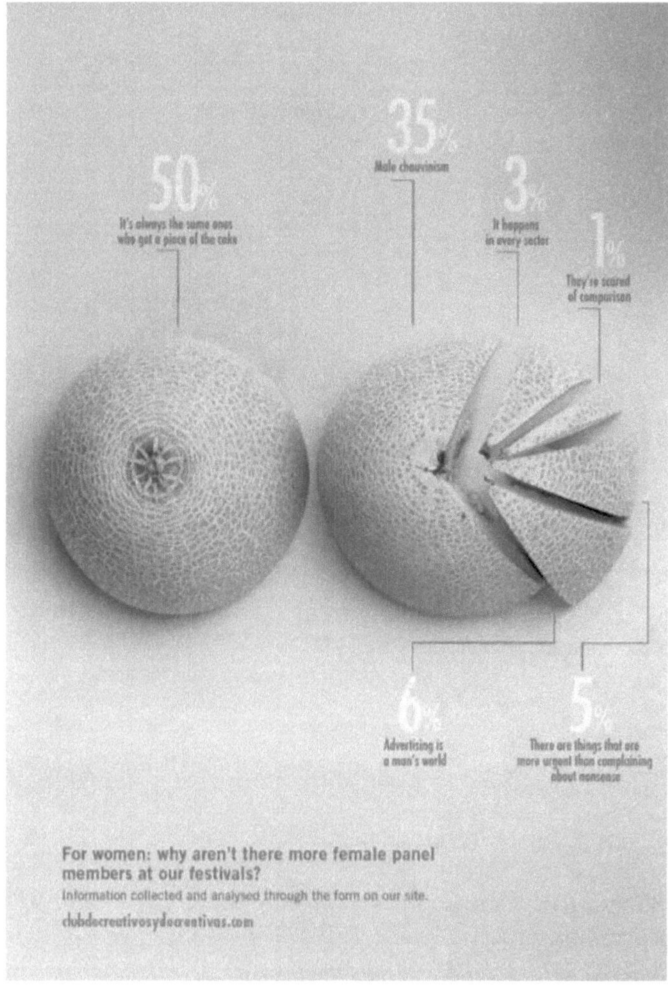

"This campaign was designed to inform rather than to judge," explain advertising agency Proximity. "We wanted to draw the advertising community's attention to gender inequality among male and female jurors at Advertising Festivals."

A great example of the maxim "Show, don't tell"

Is this the world's slimmest print ad?

When M&C Saatchi Stockholm were asked to promote LG Electronics' new curved OLED-TV they noted that it was 4mm thin - the same width as the most-read tech magazine in the Nordics, Sound & Vision. The agency cleverly capitalised on the coincidence, using the magazine spine as a unique media placement - creating what they've called 'The World's Slimmest Ad' for 'The World's Slimmest OLED-TV'.

These are some of the best ads printed around the world in 2014. What do you think is so unique about these ads?

THIS IS THE POWER OF GREAT POSITIONING!

THE ELECTRIFYING BRAIN SECRET TO MARKETING

The Triune brain model by Dr. Paul Mac Lean

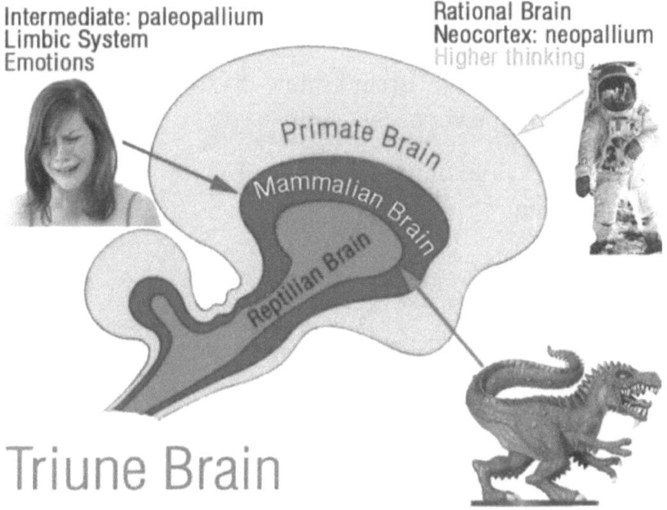

This is the most electrifying secret to understand marketing. I want you to know this secret so that you can excel the art of marketing and become a bestselling author!

Here is some interesting piece of information to put things into perspective:

- Age of earth - About 4.5 billion years

- Age of life - About 2.5 billion years

- Age of modern human - About 150,000 years

HUMANS ARE JUST A BLIP IN THE RACE AGAINST TIME!

EVOLUTION OF LIFE:

REPTILES – MAMMALS – HUMANS

According to Dr. Paul Mac Lean, the human brain has three layers:

1. Reptilian Brain: As per evolution, this is the oldest brain and almost 35 million years old.

2. Mammalian Brain/Limbic System: This is the second layer of the brain.

3. Neocortex/Rational Brain: This is the youngest brain.

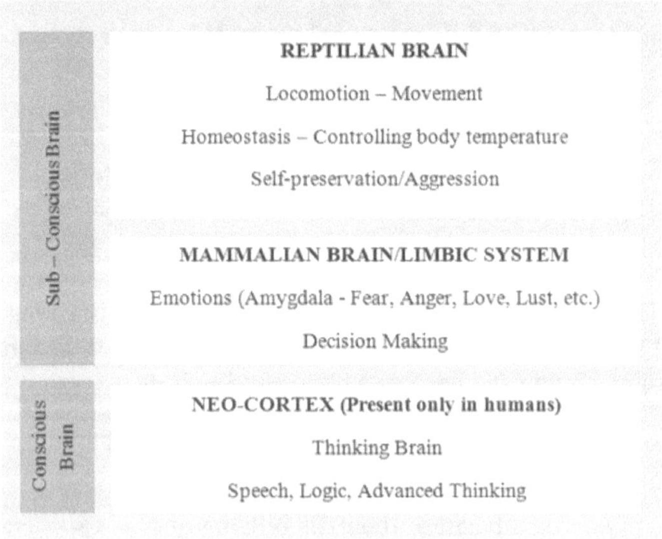

Sub – Conscious Brain

REPTILIAN BRAIN

Locomotion – Movement

Homeostasis – Controlling body temperature

Self-preservation/Aggression

MAMMALIAN BRAIN/LIMBIC SYSTEM

Emotions (Amygdala - Fear, Anger, Love, Lust, etc.)

Decision Making

Conscious Brain

NEO-CORTEX (Present only in humans)

Thinking Brain

Speech, Logic, Advanced Thinking

As you already know that humans are the youngest living beings, it is obvious that the Neocortex is the weakest brain as per evolution. According to neuroscientists, the decision-making brain, i.e., the Mammalian brain is the strongest and Amygdala, the button in this brain is responsible for all emotions.

Food for thought:

Why do you love sports, horror movies, dance and music so much? Why do people commit crimes even after knowing it's inhuman? Why is alarm, anger and fear the most prevalent? Why do you forget lyrics of a song yet remember the tune? Answer: Strongest brain is your Limbic System!

Now that you have a perspective about the human brain, let me ask you a question!

WHAT IS THE EASIEST WAY TO SELL YOUR PRODUCT TO THE CUSTOMER?

ANSWER:

IF YOU CAN AROUSE ALARM OR PASSION IN YOUR CUSTOMER ABOUT YOUR PRODUCT, YOU CAN NEVER LOSE!

HOW DO YOU DO THAT?

TARGET THE OLD BRAIN OF YOUR CUSTOMER!

MAKE THEM FEEL!

This is just an example of the kind of perspectives you will get in my sessions!

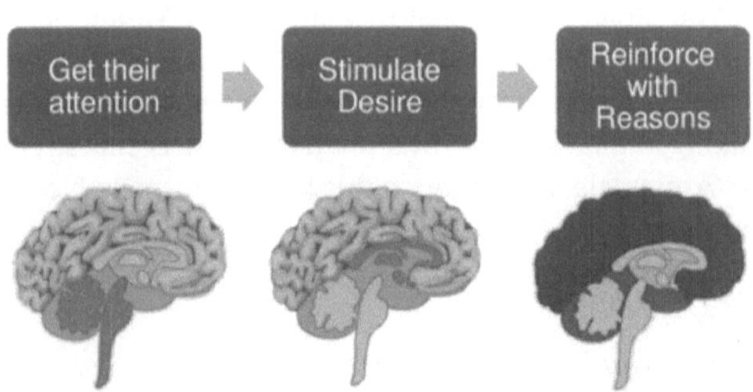
Get their attention
Stimulate Desire
Reinforce with Reasons
Three Steps to cracking the deal

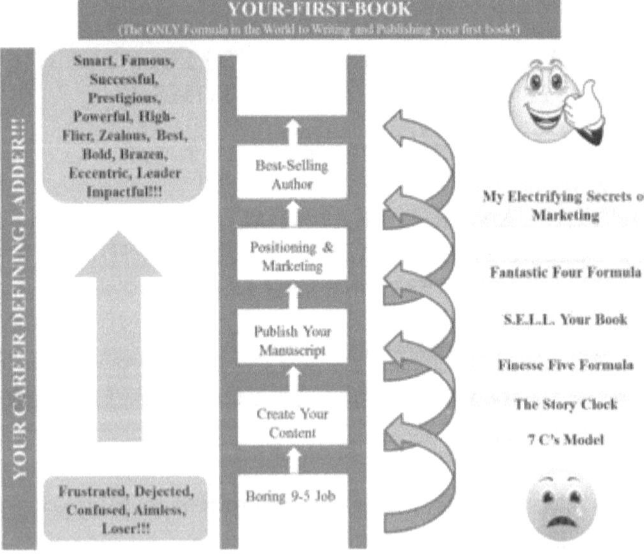
YOUR-FIRST-BOOK
(The ONLY Formula in the World to Writing and Publishing your first book!)
YOUR CAREER DEFINING LADDER!!!
Smart, Famous, Successful, Prestigious, Powerful, High-Flier, Zealous, Best, Bold, Brazen, Eccentric, Leader Impactful!!!
Best-Selling Author
Positioning & Marketing
Publish Your Manuscript
Create Your Content
Boring 9-5 Job
Frustrated, Dejected, Confused, Aimless, Loser!!!
My Electrifying Secrets of Marketing
Fantastic Four Formula
S.E.L.L. Your Book
Finesse Five Formula
The Story Clock
7 C's Model

<u>YOU NEED TO PEEL THE ONION FOR DEEP UNDERSTANDING!</u>

V.
SOLUTION

- The Day I Got Bankrupt!

It has taken me two years to reach this chapter. Yes, you got it right! The day I got bankrupt, I started implementing the RACIST hexagon to my life and things have been extraordinarily different henceforth. I guarantee that your life will turnaround completely once you too start implementing this hexagon to your life and experience what I call the *6-dimensional fever of your lifetime.*

Have you ever imagined being completely sucked down under by life's circumstances? Have you ever been treated like a door-mat by your so-called closest friends? Have you ever really made lemon juice when life threw lemons at you?

Last year in 2015, sometime around my birthday, I was travelling to Kolkata by train. I often take the train as the whole experience of meeting strangers and talking to them for hours really drives me crazy. Moreover, there is something that I feel a train can offer which a plane cannot: time to know each other (for short-distance travel of course, I'm not talking about a 21-hour flight to Boston!) I generally take the AC three-tier but this time I happened to be in the two-tier instead. Imagine gushing through a terrible Bangalore traffic and just arriving in time to catch the train on a busy Monday! Hooooo…… hoopla of an affair I tell you! I went and sat on my seat which turned out to be a passage, upper berth one (I just love these seats for some God-forsaken reason even I don't know). What would your reaction be if you suddenly realised that you are surrounded by a huge bunch of army *jawans* occupying the next five berths, so around ten of them in all. *(A few of them turned out to be real cute as well, aha, I'm interested in men, you see...)* After the evening soup was served in the Duronto Express travelling from Yeshwantpur to Howrah (thanks to Mamata Di, this train has made our lives a lot easier), I knew what I wanted to appease my senses. What is the first thought in your mind that strikes you the moment you hear the word 'Army'? Well, for someone like me who likes to indulge in stories, the first thing that struck me was 'Great Perspectives'. If you are a traveller, you definitely have stories and experiences to share, and if you are in the army, then you have both happy and sad stories, and for a storyteller like me, there is no other best friend than you.

So, I broke the ice!

"Hi, I'm Sharmin."

"Well, hello there, I'm Captain Vikramaditya Ranawat!"

(I obviously couldn't ask him what he did as it was obvious but considering his debonair and the masculine baritone with which he instantly struck my attention, I couldn't stop checking him out. The insignia of being in the army was oozing out from his eyes and I just wanted to go on talking.)

"I have been highly enthused by the Army and always wanted to join…"

"Oh, you should have, we need more women at the front. Your mental endurance levels are far higher than any man's. I respect your gender ma'am."

(Just for the record: You have no idea about the chemical reactions that were going on in my head by now. Guess I was already in love with this camouflage-suited man. No, wait, may be the absence of enough women in his league made him mark such comments. I am absolutely confident about my physical appearance. Okay, focus, focus, focus! My thoughts seemed to be digressing all over the place by now.)

After a light conversation with him about his life and after showing-off my communicating skills with a total stranger, I got to know the real incident that had struck these boys in green. Never in my abysmally low times, did I ever imagine that my love for an insanely handsome, Rajput Captain would be so short-lived. Apparently, he was travelling to Dibrugarh in Assam to get married and so a bunch of them had managed to get leaves to attend the wedding ceremony. Boy, was I shattered……

Nevertheless, as the eternally optimistic mind always feels that hope springs eternal, I chose to take the conversation ahead in the hopes of getting some real meat. He told me about his gallantry-filled life and how he was one of the youngest Captains in the history of Indian Army for his achievements in sports and social welfare. After an hour-long conversation over dinner, he asked me if I would like to see his fiancé's picture. With great abstinence, did I finally say yes! What I saw next completely shook me up from within. I was picturing an Asameese doll in my mind adorning the beautiful Mekhala Chadar, who had managed to blow away the Captain's mind with her thunderous beauty. Imagine seeing the picture of a woman whose face is half burnt and she is still smiling with great pomp and vigour! It turns out that she had been an acid attack victim. Apparently, the Captain was posted in Assam for a while and that is where they had met and fallen in love. The acid attack happened about two years ago when he was posted in Karnataka.

I had just fallen in love with him all over again. Need I say more? I was looking for perspectives and what I got in return was an epidemic called humanity with a lot of love and respect for each other. He was about to get married to a girl whose face was half-burnt and was filled with marks after six surgeries, was still recuperating from the trauma. All I remember is he telling me, "I really love her, you know. She didn't want to marry me because of her scars but I never left her. We are finally getting married in three days."

Now you must be wondering why I took the great pain of narrating the entire story of a Captain I met over a train journey to you. The one and only reason being: There is still hope for humanity. The world is not that bad a place.

Let me narrate to you another story that took me aback. I was travelling from Indira Nagar to Koramangala one evening in an Uber cab when the driver happened to strike a conversation with me. His name was Shiva as it showed on the Uber app. He asked me what I felt about the Syrian war and about the people displaced from their country. Did they have a future? How would these refugees survive the cold European winters with meagre supplies and hardly any refuge? He then asked if I knew about the deaths and displacement statistics of people in Syria? So being the tech savvy generation, I opened up Google to check the statistics. Even before my 3G could explode me with the results, Shiva said "over 300,000 have died in Syria in the last five years. More than 7 million have been internally displaced and more than 5 million have fled the country becoming refugees. The population of Bengaluru is about 8 million. Can you imagine what we would do if more than half the city was displaced by terrorism? Are we really doing our bit to support our own species?"

Yes, I know what you must be thinking. Shiva is just a driver who happens to be class 6 pass from a village in Tamil Nadu. Now I am an author and entrepreneur with two books, two companies, have travelled to 21 states across India, but I still lack what this person had just amazed me with: the time to think and express his concern about his fellow human being...!

Here is one final encounter that I feel you should know about:

At about 18:05 pm (approx.) on a Friday:

Auto driver: "Madam, madam, where do you want to go? Excuse me, excuse me ma. We are at KFC Indira Nagar. Where should I drop you?"

Traffic policeman: "Hello madame, where do you have to gooa? From 15 mins, you are here only. So much he tried to wake you, no reply banta! Did he drug youaa? Why sleeping so muchha? So muchcha traffic caused because of youaa. Do you need helpaa??? All ladies scolding poor auto manaa!! You tell me if anything wrong-doing he, I am policemanaa! I will catch him by the collar and beat him up-downaa and take him to police stationaa!"

Woman (drowsy): (To traffic policeman:) "Huh? What? Who are you? (To auto driver:) Why KFC? Who asked you to get me at KFC? Take the right to 80 feet road and step onto Thippasandra market lane. I have to go there."

5 minutes later:

Woman apologises to the crowd for the chaos.

("No worries, thank you so much for your support, I'm really sorry for the mess.")

Auto-driver drives away with a smile and humility.

(P.S.: I wasn't stoned, only sleep deprived! I felt sorry about the onward traffic on 100 feet road, Indira Nagar that I had caused.)

Why do you think I narrated these instances to you?

Each of the three instances talks about the common man of this country and their simple yet impactful stories. How many of us even get to know about these people or their lives? Which news channel or medium of communication brings out these untold stories to the world?

So, I had promised Shiva that I would do whatever little I can for my fellow beings because we all stand united against the enemies of humanity. But the question was how? I decided to ask people on social media and then do something about it using their views. So, I ran a Facebook campaign wherein I explained the whole incident followed by a plea which read as below:

"I have decided to write to the United Nations on behalf of every one of us expressing our concern about Syria and a plausible solution to the migrant crisis. I would request you all to give me your suggestions on how to interface the underprivileged with the brighter side of humanity. Will you help me in my efforts in bringing everyone together to fight for a singular cause called HUMANITY? Will you please share this post on your profile to get as many views as possible? I want to keep my promise to Shiva. But

I can't do this alone. I need your help. The world awaits your views because the people of Syria deserve YOUR SUPPORT! Please send me an email at xyz@gmail. com (original email-id withheld)..."

Now, you must be wondering that I would have received a lot of replies with suggestions loaded and people expressing their views. Well, yes, I received three hundred mails from people I had never heard of or known in my life but unfortunately half of them did not even know about the Syrian crisis. About ten of them came up with some suggestions and the rest were just criticising me for concentrating on Syria when there is a huge electricity problem in Bangalore alone.

I was taken aback…

Now let me tell you an entirely different situation and then connect the dots with our above problem. Unfortunately, the education system in India does not encourage a very creative proposition, as a result of which our parents need us to focus more on our curriculum books rather than fiction/non-fiction books. Writing stories and becoming a professional writer does not deem a profession in India due to our traditional mind-set to a large extent. Hence, there is a huge gap when it comes to expressing oneself verbally and expressing his thoughts on paper. Cracking the Reading Comprehension section on the GMAT seems like a daunting task by millions due to the same reason again. If a child in his/her early days is emphasized to focus and practice on reading and writing stories more, then this problem can be solved easily.

I soon realised that there is no lack of voice or opinion in this country but there is a huge lack of the right platform where you can voice out your opinion. Imagine if you could start voicing out your opinions from the time you were twelve or thirteen years old and were sane enough to choose between the right and the wrong, what an impact you could bring to the world's largest democracy! This was exactly my thought when I started a revolution called **Penpower! Penpower is my effort in creating a small difference to humanity by giving you the power of an author! Now you too can feel the power of an author by expressing your opinions freely on this story-telling social network that aims at connecting people from all over the world in hundred+ languages.**

I started Penpower (thepenpower.com is the official website) in November 2015.

Penpower is my life's only dream and I have implemented the R.A.C.I.S.T hexagon to this concept. You must be wondering that I just went on blabbering jargons for so long but did not really explain how to actually implement this hexagon. So here is the way:

After I decided that I wanted to start a full-fledged company to support my dream and pursue my entrepreneurial interest through an actual start-up, I had two options to choose from: One, build an NGO-like platform which would be open-source and crowd-funded, second, run a healthy, flourishing business to not just impact lives but in-turn create a mark in the history of story-telling! I chose the latter.

I started Penpower on my own back in November 2015. Due to shortage of funds, I could not afford to hire web developers, designers and writers for me. Hence, I decided to outsource the technology to a start-up in Koramangala, Bangalore. I did the basic UI/UX design and then they built a minimum viable product (MVP) for me. In the meantime, I had multiple opportunities to pitch and attend a number of start-up events to raise seed funding for my start-up. I had applied to twenty-two seed-funds including VC firms that invested in early-stage start-ups. Then a friend suggested writing to angel investors directly through Linked-in and I sat and wrote to ninety-five angel investors across India, sending them requests on Linked-in. To my surprise exactly ninety-one accepted my requests, out of which only forty-five replied to my messages. Now I don't exactly know if the ninety-one converts were because I am a woman or if they actually liked my idea! However, the forty-five sincerely asked me to send my deck to them with the funds required and the projection details mentioned on the last sheet. I finally ended up meeting sixteen of them in Bangalore, Mumbai and Delhi. *(Just for the record: My sincere habits of recording everything on an excel sheet and saving it for future reference gives me the exact details as mentioned above.)* Ten of them turned me down saying the idea won't work or it's too early to invest and that they needed more traction. All of this happened in early January 2016 and by now we had around 1000+ stories on the platform. The remaining six asked me to either wait or follow-up in the next two months as they had to secure funds before looking into this one. And thanks to the fall of the E-commerce world, a lot of them had secured heavy losses. So basically, I had achieved the Wikipedia of angel investors and VCs on my Linked-in by the end of January 2016!

But soon the problem of shortage of funds arose as there were maintenance charges that had to be taken care of. I even needed some funds for marketing and promoting the platform. My credit card bills utilised a majority of my savings and I was at a near-broke condition where I couldn't even manage to pay my house rent. I had practically reached a riches-to-rags condition. One day I just got bankrupt! I had no choice but take up a remote job to support my dream and my basic expenses. I didn't have the money to even buy milk or bread, let alone travelling to office. I didn't have a choice but swipe the credit card again for my food needs. I took up a content writer job for a start-up who felt it was way below my level because they were bootstrapped and wouldn't be able to pay me much. Well, all I was looking for was a basic salary to enable my dream.

Meanwhile, something really exciting happened. One of my friends had recommended my name to one of the food start-up founders for an exotic position at his start- up. I guess probably after going through my Wikipedia pages and researching about the volume of work I had done in the last few years, mainly on the marketing side, this founder offered me the position of Chief Marketing Officer at his Series B funded start-up for a salary of 25 Lakhs per annum. Hold your horses: I obviously refused! He asked me if I needed more money and I just politely sent him the below text: "Thanks for the offer mate, but I have to run my own start-up. I shall see you in the field someday. Good luck!" Imagine the amount of arrogance in this one statement of mine and then the very next minute all of it getting flushed when I receive a text with my credit card dues for the following month! But I have had no regrets so far!

In February 2016, I happened to meet the Managing Director of a very renowned VC firm in India. By now, I had practically understood one thing: the only thing that sells without any dual thoughts and bigotry is your self-confidence. Even after a number of rejections and let downers, my confidence was absolutely unfazed. I walked into his office as if he was my best buddy. After waiting for about ten minutes, I was directed to a conference room where the MD and his team of two people were waiting to meet me. For the first time, my heart did not skip any beats. This just seemed like an everyday affair to me. After a brief introduction, I began presenting my idea to the team and spoke non-stop for almost half an hour. The MD just got up and left.

I was still unabashed. My heart did not sink because I was kind of getting used to the frequent rejections by now. After two minutes, the MD walked in with a bottle of packaged water for me and these were his exact words, "Sharmin, I have never heard a better speaker than you in my life. Your passion, enthusiasm and dynamic attitude has completely blown me away. I want to meet your team next week."

I'm sure by now you would have understood the sudden boost that my head was filled with. I got my team the next week and had an hour-long conversation which ended with a unique statement, "We are 90 per cent done, Sharmin! You just need to meet our Chairman and then we would be good to go."

It was the month of March when I happened to finally meet the Chairman, almost two and a half weeks after my last meeting. One evening I got a call from the MD's assistant and I was asked if I were free the next morning for a meeting. It was so sudden and unplanned that I was not prepared at all, though I could not afford to miss this opportunity as it was happening after a long wait. So, I agreed to meet him.

I walked into his office the next day, dressed in complete formals, with a slight hesitation, I wonder why. Had you been with me, you would have seen 30 feet by 15 feet (approx.) office on the fifth floor of a commercial building at one of the poshest locales of Bangalore. The Chairman was on a phone call and CNBC business news was playing on the probable 52 inch LED screen, mounted on the wall in front of where he sat. I also noticed a number of books behind on the shelf, most of them being business books. Since he was on the call, I picked up a book, titled 'The Snowball: Warren Buffet and the Business of Life' by Alice Schroeder. As I was reading all praises about Buffet and how unnecessary spending should be avoided, the Chairman put the phone receiver down and looked at me as I had been sitting for almost 15 minutes in front of him, though he didn't look at me even once.

"I heard a lot of praises about you. Let's see if you're really worth my time. What are you trying to build exactly?"

I was so awestruck with that arrogance in his tone that I began sharing my thoughts with him. For some reason, I was still hesitant about the air in that space. Something just did not feel right to me. In the next three minutes, he interrupted and asked two questions in an even more arrogant tone. He then jumped to his conclusion that this idea wouldn't work and that I shouldn't be raising funds. Rather, I should get a job and continue self-funding for the next one year at least.

His body language and tone could be defined in just two words: ARROGANCE GALORE!

I was distressed. I was upset. I was angry.

I got up and left. As I was about to enter the lift, someone called from behind and I turned. It was the MD.

"Sharmin, listen, I heard what the Chairman said. I have to tell you that I am still with you and am willing to support you in whatever way I can. Take some time off, decide on how you want to take your business ahead and let's connect soon."

I thanked him for his generosity and left.

For the first time did I cry in an auto while going back home. I really cried.

I went bonkers for the next two weeks not knowing what was happening. I was probably struck by mental carnage.

It was during this time that I happened to meet an old friend at a bar one day. He was enjoying a drink with another friend of his. We got introduced and began talking. It turned out that he was a Tech guru. We exchanged numbers. I needed a Chief Technology Officer for my start-up, so I was desperately hunting for a like- minded individual. I happened to have a telephonic conversation with this new-found friend called Ratan Chandrashekharan, hailing from Dharvad, a district in Karnataka in South India. After a discussion about his technical expertise, I wanted to know a bit about his personal life as well. What I heard next completely jolted me to bits and pieces! He said and I quote, *"Arey Sharmin, hamare father toh farmer the, kisan pata hai na aapko. Sabzi ugate the. Aloo, tamatar, gajar wagera. Chalis saal ke the jab aisa sukha pada, na bearish na kuch, aur sar par itna loan. Kya karte bichare, mar gaye. Mar kya gaye, system ne maar dala. Aur apne piche chod gaye paitees saal ki widhwa aur do chote bete."* His tone was this blatant throughout the conversation. He was so calm and composed that his composure psyched me out. You know what he said? "Don't be angry Sharmin. I was angry too but I learnt it very early in life that you need to channelize your anger to fruition because **your anger is your greatest enemy and also your best friend.**"

Ratan is a Computer Science graduate from IIT Kharagpur and his younger brother studies at the UCLA in the USA.

Have you ever heard a farmer's story from his own son with such humility?

Because I was distraught, I decided to do something about it as my friend Ratan asked me to. So, I wrote an email to the Managing Director of the VC firm I had had an interaction with two weeks back.

Dear Sir,

Apologies for the delay in responding to you. I was trying to do something very constructive after my last stint with the Chairman. I must say that I love people who can challenge me because there aren't too many who can, though I would have appreciated it more, had he been more constructive rather than critical. Like I always take a look at any situation in life, below is a brief update:

(Just for the record: "I am not trying to justify my anonymity, just putting things into perspective my way")

Why the two weeks' delay? **('Time and tide have always waited for me.')**

I sat down in introspection thinking what exactly had gone wrong. I actually took a break from everything and just sat at home. One thing that the Chairman said was to continue self-funding by taking up a job. Well, it had been four years that I'd quit my job, so I was a little apprehensive if anyone would offer me one. However, I decided to give it a try. To my surprise, when the first company I applied to, read my name and profile as - Founder and CEO, thepenpower.com on LinkedIn, called me immediately, offering me the post of Co-Founder (Chief Marketing Officer, precisely) with 5% stocks at his funded start-up with a salary of 1 Lakh per month. Of course, this super-boosted my already high levels of confidence. But I was too curious to find out that without even interviewing/meeting me why he was offering me the job. So, I called him. It turns out that he has been one of the maximum content contributors on thepenpower.com and that he feels I am one of the craziest women alive with a great business idea sprawling to be the next big thing. He said he would be honoured if I were to join their team.

(P.S.: You can well imagine what I was feeling at that point of time. No, I'm not driven by emotions at all…)

What did I do next? **('The curious case of time–bound criticism')**

Well of course I had no intentions of joining another company. I sat down and revamped my entire positioning and created a whole new pitch deck with intensive details like my plan for the next six months, marketing plans, infrastructure plans, met and interviewed a lot of people whom I wanted to join my company, showered people with my leadership skills and regained all that I had lost in the last 45- minute meeting.

How am I going to enable things in the future? **('From Aspirins to Aspirations, I'm unstoppable!')**

So, coming to the most important section out of all: Everyone can talk but only a few can actually implement. I had a chat with *ABC (name withheld)* also who is very keen on getting updates and discussing things forward. Here is the plan:

I am seeking 25 Lakhs funding for an 8% equity in my company, i.e., a post-money valuation of 3.125 Crores. I have a full length plan in place with a lot of things sorted out unlike the last time. Let us have a discussion now when you are free and take things forward.

Look forward to hearing from you.

Regards,

Sharmin

He replied in the next one hour that he would like to meet me the following week.

So, I went. This continued for the next two months. However, nothing fruitful could be gained as there were not too many investors to come on board. However, we continue being in touch till date.

In the meanwhile, two investors who I had connected with in the past, suddenly got back and wanted to meet me. One of them was from Mumbai and he wanted me to come down and meet him for a face-to-face meeting. I went with my co-founder to the Coffee Day at Hiranandani, Mumbai to meet this person.

After taking him through the deck and explaining the classics of the trade, he said, "Sharmin, I love your idea and presentation and I see you have a good team in place. But I would like to ask you that when do you plan to get married?"

"I'm sorry, what?"

"See, let me explain. I think you should step down as CEO and let your co-founder take over that position."

If all the existing drama wasn't enough, this was the salt on my wound, the perfect icing on the cake. This time it wasn't about me or my company, rather, about my gender. Suddenly the woman inside was hurt.

"Sir, if you are looking for a man to be the CEO, then let me tell you, SHE'S THE MAN. If there is anyone meant to be, it's her or no one else for this job", said my co-founder and long-time friend!

I was elated with joy at how lucky I was to have such a backbone behind my journey. We thanked him for his time and left.

I was back to Bangalore again, this time to meet the second investor who had been messaging me for quite some time now, expressing a huge amount of interest in my company.

After a set of meetings with this second investor, he agreed to invest along with another friend of his, a sum of $100,000 US. So finally, the day came when I went to sign the term sheet.

Starbucks, Indiranagar, Bangalore (They had just opened that place):

"I like your business plan a lot and also appreciate your team's dedication and energy. But before signing the term sheet, I would like to discuss something really important."

"Sure Sir. You probably want to revisit the projected numbers again, I have an updated ex..."

"No Sharmin, I don't need to see any more sheets. I wanted to talk about you. Look, I've been thinking a lot about you lately, I find you very attractive. I would like to hook up with you. How about a weekend getaway to Goa? I shall book us the best suite at the Park Hyatt Resort in Goa. We can sign the deal over a bottle of champagne once we are back. What do you say?"

"Ummm… (flabbergasted literally) Thanks for the offer, but I'm not interested."

"What happened Sharmin, why not?" (By now I was almost losing it…)

"Because I'm not attracted to you Sir, that's why."

"But I thought you are a very outgoing girl and would want to do things spontaneously."

"Of course, I am. But that doesn't mean I hook up against my will. Anyway, thanks for your time. Have a good day Sir."

"Listen, how serious are you about your company? I can take you places."

"I'm very serious Sir but no, thank you!"

"If ever you wish to reconsider, then you know I'm just a phone call away Sharmin…"

(With a smile)

"Never mind Sir, thank you!"

Have you ever imagined the quantum of pain that a woman goes through during child birth? Did you know that the sum total of the pain a woman bears throughout her lifetime during menstruation is much more than the pain during a single child birth? Do you know there is one pain that beats everything else: the pain a woman CEO goes through during her entrepreneurial journey!

YES, I JUST GOT PROPOSITIONED…!

The next thing I remember I got typhoid and was admitted in the hospital. One week later, I heard some terrible news, a fellow entrepreneur friend had committed suicide because of depression, though I don't know the real reason. If all of this weren't enough, something even more horrendous happened in my personal life that I do not wish to talk about at this juncture. Someone really close to me gave me the greatest gift on my birthday, a news that shook me from within and I was left completely alone. He left me saying he couldn't handle my extreme emotions anymore…

I went bankrupt in the truest sense!

I had never been this depressed in my life ever! My 28th birthday, possibly the worst birthday ever! What a gift!

In the interim, I got an invite to speak at the TEDx Dumas followed by TEDx MITP in October. I went against all mental odds and spoke in front of a huge audience at both the events. Below are a few snippets from the event:

TED
x
Dumas

I got a standing ovation at both the platforms. But, only I know how I kept my cool with that fake smile, thanking everyone for their generosity and considering me worth this incredible platform.

I was going through mental claustrophobia, I believe. My very good friend Angela came to my rescue and finally took me to a psychologist to fight the so-called depression I was going through! After great hesitation, I agreed to visit the counsellor. Yes, I did therapy. I realised I should have gone earlier. Counselling isn't that bad after all. I went home and stayed there for Christmas and New Year's. I never let anyone get an iota of doubt about what I was going through.

(Guess after reading all this, my near and dear ones are going to be in for a lot of shock…)

I came back in January 2017. The first thing I did was get rid of all the negativity and started writing and reading a lot again. I wrote a play and did four runs, got back in full vigour to feel pumped up again.

One of the days, when I was out with a few friends at a nearby pub in Koramanagala, very close to the Sony World Signal, where I stay, I suddenly bumped into an old friend of mine after three years. We had spoken only thrice in the last three years and out of that, I had called twice. He was more of a reclusive person, also a voracious reader. I didn't know what was coming next. He turned out to be the silver lining in my cloud. Next, I remember, sitting down with him and talking continuously for the next five hours. We spoke about everything under the sky: start-ups, capitalism, terrorism, Kashmir, World Wars, Relationships, Human race, Evolution, marketing and what not! It turned out that this guy was a marketing genius!

I have to say this: This guy gave me mental orgasms with his ocean of knowledge in these five hours. After a very long time, did I actually meet someone who read as much as I did. We debated, discussed, argued, yelled and then said CHEERS! Wow, I felt ecstatic again! The best thing he told me was, "Sharmin don't give a f***, you should always keep a f***!" I asked him to explain that to which he replied, "Don't give a f*** about unnecessary things in your life. You should keep and own f***s like a bottle of vintage wine, an Ayn Rand book, the wildest memory ever, an explosive orgasm, a great friend, an impact upon people, a collection of the best IMDB movies, a trip to Antarctica and the world, etc."

He made me understand that smartness lies in realising your mistakes and moving on. So, I decided to scrap thepenpower.com. I read the book 'Positioning', 'Rotten Rejections' and 'Finding Freedom' as he had suggested.

What came alive was:

Instoried.com (Lynda.com for written communication using AI)

Of course, I'm not a virgin! How could I be? I had just reproduced my baby under a different brand!

I was awarded the Build India Award for exceptional work as a woman entrepreneur on the 12th March 2017 at the India International Centre, New Delhi.

INSIGNIA

(THE RACIST ME!)

R (Rebellious): My rebellious attitude led me to build Instoried.com against all odds. In fact, this platform Instoried.com is built on a rebellious note itself: INSTAGRAM FOR STORIES!

A (Aspirational): My aspirations to reach and impact a million lives led me to becoming a woman who is unfazed and undeterred by the so-called callous circumstances that I was surrounded with for so long.

C (Contrasting): What is the greatest contrast of the world today? Too many problems, too less solutions! Do you really think there isn't a solution to climate change or the migrant crisis or terrorism? Of course, there is! Then where is the problem? The problem lies in the fact that our voices do not reach our leaders who make decisions on behalf of us. What is the solution to bridge this gap? I built a whole business around the world's greatest contrast: You are the solution, you the people! Instories is of the people, for the people and by the people!

(Food for thought: Why do you think I gave such a contrasting name to this book?)

I (Imperfect): I am imperfect! I am imperfect! I am imperfect! This is the reason I continuously strive towards perfection. But I'm never satisfied. If I'm working at speed X today, I strive to work at speed 2X tomorrow to reach my goal.

S (Sensational): I am an emotional person but there is no place for any negative emotions in my life. I'm only driven by good, positive emotions. We all have needs, but getting your priorities right and channelizing your negative energies in a positive way, is an art that I have learnt the difficult way in life. The moment I started implementing this art to my life, the right balance was automatically struck. The fruits I've yielded so far have been sensational.

T (The High-Flier): What is the biggest problem that our youth is facing today? Lack of employment? Being an entrepreneur and a job-creator automatically puts you on the pedestal and you belong to the High-Flying league.

EPILOGUE

I have been extremely fortunate to have trained hundreds of individuals and helped them fulfil their biggest dream of writing their first book. Here are a few excerpts from some of my students:

BM Poonacha (CEO, Real Estate Heroes)

For a very long time, I had been planning to write a book because I feel writing a book is the only way I could reach out to a large number of audiences. Incidentally I happened to meet Sharmin about 1.5 years ago for some other purpose. I recently asked her if she could write a book for me. She was shocked and she said, "Why do you want me to write a book for you when you can yourself create your own masterpiece?" I was surprised because I had no time and idea about how to put across my thoughts. So, she told me about her program 'Your-First-Book'. I couldn't believe that there could be a full-fledged product on writing a book! So out of curiosity, I decided to attend this course. What turned out next was the most blasphemous thing I had ever imagined! Picture this! You attend a course and then your manuscript is ready within a month! Need I say more! This is highly recommended for any person who wants to write a book and become a published author! Sharmin is one woman who has the power to change the way you look at life!

Cover page of Poonacha's first book

Arun Nair (IT Professional)

I have been working as a software engineer for the last 6 years in Bangalore, living a very mundane life with the usual 9-hour work schedule. Writing has always been a very distant dream to me. I would write and tear and never collect anything. I heard about Sharmin from a friend of mine, who suggested talking to her once about how to write a book. I never thought I could meet her as she was a very established person by then. But she turned out to be the humblest and the most encouraging individual I have ever met. After completing the course with her, I got a very structured model to writing and I could see my dream come true. She is an expert in brain science and understands the reader's brain very well. I have already completed close to 100 pages of my manuscript. Sharmin gave wings to my dream and I feel like a bird ready to fly. Thank you Sharmin!

Cover page of Arun's first book

Vishal Upadhyay (Ex-Banker with a Fortune 100 Bank, New-Delhi)

Last year I took a sabbatical from work as I wanted to expand my horizons to fulfil my passion for writing and write something which would get published. However, I didn't have the guidance and every time I thought about it, I failed miserably. I was always bogged down by the idea of getting a book published in India as it seems to be next to impossible for a common man. That is when I chanced upon Sharmin at a seminar and I decided to join her classes. I never knew that writing could be so easy. You don't have to pursue a course in journalism or literature to be a writer. What you need is Sharmin's models to write your book. Sharmin has a unique way of conducting her classes where she has developed a number of models to understand the science of writing. In the first class itself, I could see a difference in my content and then by the end of the course, there was a hugely distinct transformation in my style of writing. I recommend these classes for any budding authors who are confused about how to start. Sharmin not only talks about why, what and how you should write a book, but she offers a 360-degree angle toward the business of writing. She also talks about how to publish your book. The most surprising thing is that her models are based on brain science and positioning!

Lakshmi Naidu (CEO, GJ Solutions and PR expert)

Your-First-Book is the most revolutionary product of this century! It is a step-by-step process to writing your story and getting it published. This is a sheer breakthrough in the field of literature.

Joseph Pulikkottil (Vice-President, Citibank, Founder of NGO and Philanthropist)

I have been working with Citibank for a very long time. After 12 years of work, I finally decided to take a break and move out to do what I really wanted to do. I have been always very interested about Science and Economics. I used to read about them a lot and always wanted to write something different from the regular stereotype jargon. In the meantime, I met Sharmin through a common friend. Our first conversation took place over the phone. The kind of perspectives she gave me over the phone made me feel that if there were one person who can drive me to achieve the impossible, then that was her and only her. She was so influential that after our first talk itself, I was sure about soon completing my first book. She not only taught me how to write a book but also the secrets of marketing it. She gave such mind-blowing ways to market and promoting my book that I was amazed. I have already started writing my first book titled 'Grey Matter Dialogues' and all thanks to Sharmin. She is 26 and truly, age is just a number. There is no age to impact lives. Thank you Sharmin for such an amazing impact on my life!

Cover page of Joseph's first books

If you wish to reach me then you can contact me directly on my website http://sharminali.com/ and I shall be happy to impact your life in whatever little way I possibly can.

NOTES

In his Pulitzer prize winning work, 'The Dragons of Eden', astrophysicist, polymath and my favourite author Carl Sagan says, "To write a book on a subject so far from one's primary training is at best incautious. But the temptation was irresistible." This page has been left blank intentionally, as this is an original work and I have not referred to any material, in any way, whatsoever.

However…

… We don't exist in isolation. I had hardly read any books during my childhood besides the curriculum books given by the school. At the age of eighteen, I actually started reading and ever since, I have not stopped. So here is a list of 50 most impactful books that have influenced my thoughts and given me great perspectives over the years.

1.   The Fountainhead by Ayn Rand

2.   The Dragons of Eden by Carl Sagan

3.   The Black Swan: The Impact of the Highly Improbable by Nassim Nicholas Taleb

4.   A Whole New Mind by Daniel Pink

5.   Sapiens: A Brief History of Humankind by Yuval Noah Harari

6.   The Origin of Species by Charles Darwin

7.   Descartes' Error: Emotion, Reason and the Human Brain by Anthony Damasio

8.   Looking For Spinoza: Joy, Sorrow and the Feeling Brain by Anthony Damasio

9.   The Emotional Brain: The Mysterious Underpinnings of Emotional Life by Joseph Ledoux

10.   Synaptic Self: How Our Brains Become Who We Are by Joseph Ledoux

11.   The Myth of Mirror Neurons – The Real Neuroscience of Communication and Cognition by Gregory Hickok

12.   Hollywood Economics: How Extreme Uncertainty Shapes the Film Industry by Arthur De Vany

13.   The Millionaire Mind by Thomas Stanley

14. The Problems of Philosophy by Bertrand Russell

15. The Conquest of Happiness by Bertrand Russell

16. The Analysis of Mind by Bertrand Russell

17. Marriage and Mortals by Bertrand Russell

18. Religion and Science by Bertrand Russell

19. Against the Gods: The Remarkable Story of Risk by Peter L Bernstein

20. The Bed of Procrustes: Philosophical and Pracitical Aphorisms by Nassim Nicholas Taleb

21. The Elements of Persuasion by Richard Maxwell and Robert Dickman

22. Chance: A Guide to Gambling, Love, the Stock Market, and Just About Everything Else by Amir D. Azce

23. Predictably Irrational: The Hidden Forces that Shape Our Decisions by Dan Ariely

24. The Upside of Irrationality by Dan Ariely

25. The Art of War by Sun Tzu

26. Rethinking History by Keith Jenkins

27. From Beirut to Jerusalem by Thomas Friedman

28. On Success by Charles Munger

29. Rotten Rejections: The Letters That Publishers Wish They'd Never Sent by Andre Bernard

30. Fear: Essential Wisdom for Getting Through The Storm by Thich Nhat Hanh

31. Siddhartha by Herman Hesse

32. The Tibetan Book of Living and Dying by Sogyal Rinpoche

33. Finding Freedom by Jarvis Jay Masters

34. The Self Aware Universe by Amit Goswami

35. The Buddha in Daily Life by Richard Causton

36. How to Travel with a Salmon and Other Essays by Umberto eco

37. A History of the World in 10 ½ Chapters by Julian Barnes

38. The Clockwise Universe: Issac Newton, the Royal Society, and the Birth of the Modern World by Edward Dolnick

39. The Stranger by Albert Camus

40. The Plague by Albert Camus

41. Nausea by Jean Paul Sartre

42. We Have Only This Life to Live: The Selected Essays of Jean Paul Sartre, 1939-1975 by Jean Paul Sartre

43. Candide by Voltaire

44. The Universe in a Single Atom: The Convergence of Science and Spirituality by His Holiness The Dalai Lama

45. A History of the Mind: Evolution and the Birth of Consciousness by Nicholas Humphrey

46. The entire Human Revolution series by Dr Daisaku Ikeda

47. The entire New Human Revolution series by Dr Daisaku Ikeda

48. The Atlas Shrugged by Ayn Rand

49. Pale Blue Dot by Carl Sagan

50. Phantoms in the Brain: Probing the Mysteries of the Human Mind by Vilayanur S Ramachandran and Sandra Blakeslee

"I promise to give back to the Earth in whatever way I can…"

- Sharmin Ali

Get in touch with me at:

Personal website: sharminali.com

Twitter: @SharminAli1

Facebook: www.facebook.com/sharmin.ali.92

What People Have To Say About The Book:

"Sharmin shares how she has learnt to thrive from her experiences – those thrust upon her and those she chose! Written in her bold, catchy but easy style – this is the story of an explorer of experiences and a winner in all circumstances."

- Deepak Natraj
(MD, Aarin Capital)

"Imperfection is beauty, Madness is genius, it's better to be absolutely ridiculous than absolutely boring. The book is an epitome of this. The journey of self is depicted beautifully peppered with great anecdotes. Interesting take on the six paradigm pillars of the modern age racism. Book makes a great reading!"

- Shivoo Koteshwar
(Author, Entrepreneur & Director, Mediatek)

"Ever felt a twinge of nostalgia strike really hard? Well, this book ensures it evokes feelings of wanting to turn back the hands of time – and most importantly, relish and re-learn some of the most important yet long forgotten life lessons."

- Pooja Chandraprabhan
(Lifestyle Journalist, Deccan Chronicle)

"Naked truth, on your face - a bold story from a beautiful woman, straight from the heart."

- Sudipto Das
(Author, Speaker & Entrepreneur)

"Stupendous work. They say life is long if you know how to use it. This woman is definitely going to live long."

-Akanksha Gupta,
Marcomm Specialist

"Smart, Intelligent, Irreverent! A Must Read!"

– Anurag Srivastava,
Co-Founder, SMG & Jungle Ventures

"The writing is exquisite! Definitely packed with suspense and the tangles with her personal life experiences make this book a true pleasure to read. Personally, enjoyed the parallelism between her personal stories and lessons learned which apply to absolutely everyone very much."

*– Margarita Faikh,
Founder, Botanicah*

"Catchy and inspirational reading and a must-read for strikers!"

– Linda Obregon,
Co-Founder & CEO, FoodTure